AL MURRAY
THE PUB LANDLORD'S

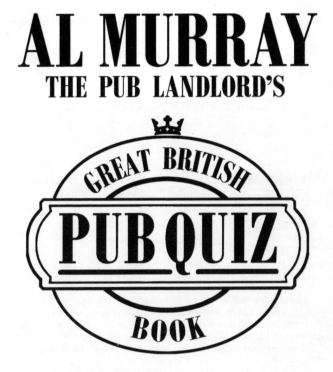

GREAT BRITISH
PUB QUIZ
BOOK

HODDER &
STOUGHTON

First published in Great Britain in 2010 by Hodder & Stoughton
An Hachette UK company

1

Copyright © Al Murray 2010

The right of Al Murray to be identified as the Author of the Work has been asserted by
him in accordance with the Copyright, Designs and Patents Act 1988.

A CIP catalogue record for this title is available from the British Library.

ISBN 978 1 444 71584 2

Typeset in Excelsior by Hewer Text UK Ltd, Edinburgh

Printed and bound by Clays Ltd, St Ives plc

Hodder & Stoughton policy is to use papers that are natural,
renewable and recyclable products and made from wood grown in sustainable
forests. The logging and manufacturing processes are expected to conform
to the environmental regulations of the country of origin.

Hodder & Stoughton Ltd
338 Euston Road
London NW1 3BH

www.hodder.co.uk

Contents

The Pub Quiz: A British Invention, of course

There is not a single person in the British Isles who has not attended a pub quiz. Now, I don't know if this is true or not, but it seems it, and if it isn't, by the time this book has gone out to bookshops around the country and into people's homes it will be true. Because the pub quiz is at the heart of the very fabric that makes up the centre of the middle of what makes Great Britain the powerhouse of the world that it is. Because it is all about questions. And their answers. Obviously. Keep up, we've only just started.

To be honest with you I am generally suspicious of questions, and you should be too. (If the very next thing you thought was 'Why?', congratulations, you are a smartarse who thinks too much and I am therefore suspicious of you too.) People asking questions tend to be policemen, social workers or, worse still, working for insurance companies (always try and make it look electrical). Intelligent people ask questions all the time, and they're not happy, are they? But pub quiz questions are OK, because they're the type of questions that have answers, the kind of questions that won't upset the mental applecart.

There are lots of types of questions: What questions, Why questions, When questions, How questions, Where questions, Who questions. They can serve the useful function of allowing you to figure out what on earth happened the night before. As in: What did I drink last night? Why did I drink so much of it? How did I drink so much of it? Where am I? Who the hell are you? But the What, Why, When, How, Where, Who questions, however, can also be used to win you stuff in pub quizzes. Because they are honest questions, with honest answers, they offer certainty in a world of doubt. You might not know if the bank your house is mortgaged with is going to go tits up, or whether that horse you bet this month's pay on will win, but you do know that Prague is the capital of the Czech Republic.

The French, of course, love questions, with their qu'est-ce que c'est? and their quelle heure est-il? and their quelle temps fait-il? and their comment appel-tu? and their comment ça va? and their ou est la gare? This is a direct consequence of their fondness for coffee, which has driven them to question everything. Mind you, if I was French I would be asking myself 'What's the point?' too. Not that there'd ever be an answer that would satisfy the restless, tortured mind of a British man trapped in the body of a Frenchman (they'd have to offer to fix *that* on the NHS). In this country we don't really like to ask questions, but we love answering them.

So it comes as no surprise to me, and I'm sure it won't to those of you familiar with me, when I tell you that the pub quiz is a British invention. It is as British as football, afternoon tea, postage stamps and underdog status. As British as Spitfires. As British as the pub itself. (No one else has pubs: they do their drinking in bars, cafes, clubs, dens, dives, halls, cellars, hovels, hammocks, caves, speakeasies, benches, secret societies, lodges, frat houses, car parks, coaches, tents, huts, shacks, air raid shelters, spas, swimming pools, ranches, luxury resorts, capsules, teepees, structures made of scaffolding and corrugated iron, tree houses, dunnies, prisons, trains, cars, ships, the driver's cab on *le metro*, planes and snow holes. And they **never** hold quizzes in any of those places. Tree house quiz anyone? No, thought not.)

No one is sure who the individual was who invented the pub quiz. Regular pub quiz goers will know that the question 'Who Invented The Pub Quiz?' never comes up in a quiz. That's because no one knows, and because this being Britain, no one has tried to claim and copyright the idea (unlike the kind of chancers you get in America who claim to have invented 'Happy Birthday' and the idea of spilling coffee on themselves for profit). At least as far as I know no one's tried to, though Jeffrey Archer is suspiciously rich given how shit his books are. Furthermore, given the natural and sensible British suspicion of clever people, it is worth noting that the pub quiz is also the only situation in which anyone likes a smartarse. Geeks and nerds cling to this crumb of comfort, a crumb of comfort that makes them feel included in a nation that otherwise might shun them – one *Star Trek* question a week will bring a whole nerd hive into your pub, and while there's no longer the smell of smoke to cover the BO, their nerd money and insatiable thirst for marked-up diet soft drinks is as good as anyone else's (that's their lot though, give a nerd an inch and he'll take a parsec).

But whoever did invent the pub quiz was without a shadow of a doubt (which is quite different to the doubt of a Shadow – if Hank Marvin isn't sure about the chord you're playing on your guitar, don't worry about it, his time has passed*) British. It smells of British Thinking**. Now, British Thinking, for those of you who didn't buy the first book – for I am a published author many times – or for those of you who did buy it but only looked at the pictures, and I admit the picture of me on the loo was distracting, is the simple concept that explains this country's cutting edge of innovation, why we're one step ahead of everyone else. It's all about combining things and creating something better than those things from those things: and the pub quiz is the perfect example. It combines pubs, something everyone loves (apart from maybe our neighbours at chucking-out time, please keep the noise down when leaving), and quizzes. And everyone loves quizzes. Everyone. Why else, how else, would they put up with Vernon Kay on the telly? Because they just love to know what the answers are in *Family Fortunes*. No way on earth they'd put up with Captain SexText otherwise (actually, in the SexText military he's not made it to Captain, Corporal more like. What he singly failed to do was offer a stupendous 'a mate borrowed my phone and there was still some credit on it' excuse, as served up by Ashley Cole, the donut). And by combining

---

* The Doubt of a Member of Queen is a different matter. If Brian May isn't sure about something, listen. Especially if it's about astrophysics or guitar playing.

** As explained in my first book, *The Pub Landlord's Book of British Common Sense*. In shops then.

pubs and quizzes it offers the best of both worlds, an interface between the intellect and the most important liberating brain fuel known to man: booze.

And that's why it makes the most of and defines all that makes the British. It uses all of our finest attributes: knowledge without peer, beautiful British common sense, steel-like guts, hardened determination, and, more than anything, a huge great pair of bloody drinking legs. That's the key; if you can't keep up with the rounds, you'll never know if you've won or not. Drink up, think up. It's not the taking part …

No other nation on earth could have come up with the phenomenon that is the pub quiz. The Italians could never have invented the pub quiz, as they keep changing teams and it plays havoc with the scoring. The Spanish definitely didn't invent it as they don't go out until 11.30 at night and the pubs are shut by then, and anyway you can't think straight when you've had a late dinner. And the Germans could never have thought of the pub quiz, and let me tell you why. The Germans are ok with the questions, the questions they can handle. It's the answers they can't grasp, because they are simply too unpalatable. Who won the First World War? Who won the Second World War? Who won the World Cup in 1966? Who invented the pub quiz? You see why they struggle?

Your classic pub quiz, like your classic healthy diet, is made up of five basic groups. The healthy diet is of course made up of crisps, nuts, scratchings, chips and the ploughman's, while your pub quiz should include music, TV and film, history, geography and sport. There's a simple reason for this. It's because we invented them all. There's no doubt in my mind: Queen invented music and they were British. History is British, your Bible's in English and that's the oldest history book in the world. We also invented all sports: football, darts, snooker, cricket, rugby and golf (we were nothing to do with sumo or kabbadi, but you can keep those as far as I'm concerned). The British came up with telly, and words like hill, mountain and river are all English words, hence we invented geography. And if you insist on having science in a pub quiz, the British invented gravity, the train and split the atom (though we got an over-keen New Zealander to do it for us – it was really dangerous) and Jean-Luc Picard* in *Star Trek* is British too**.

That we invented the pub quiz explains everything. It's the perfect pastime for the common man that involves him, yet doesn't involve chest pains and wheezing (at least not since the smoking ban). Not for us the Roman circus with its savagery and bloodletting; nor the existential pointlessness of playing bowls in gravel like they do in France; neither do we send men into arenas to fight cattle like in Spain (we have no row with the cow); to be a free man in this country we do not need to carry a firearm like our Yankee cousins; nor yet still is our national ego so fragile like the Australian that we pin our entire identity and self esteem on our national cricket team (little point, frankly); no, the British common man would sooner pit his wits against the all-knowing question master and his microphone to win a frozen chicken.

So, if you want to enjoy the best that this country has to offer in the manner of entertainment and pastime, here it is. The Great British Pub Quiz. In a book. (With answers overleaf).

---

* French name!

** That's your lot, nerds.

1 Music

1 During mating season, when foxes are in the act of coitus, they omit a bone-shuddering and blood-curdling screech that is often mistaken for the sound of a cat being brutally murdered. But who is the lead singer of Duran Duran?

2 It's widely recognised that a tone exists between 5 and 9 hertz known as the 'brown note', which is capable of making humans lose control of their bowels and can induce vomiting and diarrhoea due to rectal and oesophageal muscular spasms. This tone is often emitted from the vocal cords of the lead singer of Duran Duran, but what is his name?

3 Ringo Starr is known as the 'Underwater Beatle' due not only to the hits 'Yellow Submarine' and 'Octopus' Garden', but also to his penchant for spending thousands of pounds on diving watches. I would like to know Ringo's real name?

4 Despite Ringo's efforts, Paul McCartney's song 'Maxwell's Silver Hammer' is by far and away the worst song the Beatles ever released. It's embarrassing for everyone involved and is often blamed for splitting the band up. On which album does it feature?

5 Coldplay look like four startled meerkats, frightened by an oncoming album deadline. No one really knows the names of any of them, apart from the singer. With that in mind, what is the name of the bassist?

Answers

1 Simon Le Bon. Le Bon's vocal style is often likened to that of the mating fox and rightly so.

2 Simon Le Bon. Most of the notes that Duran Duran curl out can be described as brown.

3 Richard Starkey. Ringo released his fifteenth studio album in January 2010; it was entitled *Y Not*. He then listened back to it and realised he'd answered his own question.

4 *Abbey Road.*

5 Guy Berryman. You might not know of him, because he hasn't married a Hollywood actress and doesn't make a thing of drawing on his hands.

2 World War Two Dates

. . . .

World War Two is the cataclysmic event that shaped the world and the way we live today more than anything else, even England winning the World Cup in 1966, and any decent honest-to-goodness punter should know the crucial dates that shaped the world. Shame on anyone who doesn't know these. Bonus points for what day of the week it was.

1 It is well known that the British won the Second World War on our own, no help from no one else, and it is also an incontrovertible fact that the Germans started it – no excuses – but when did Great Britain declare war on Germany after they had started it?

2 Everyone knows the Americans came into the war two years late when they were caught out, trousers down, completely by surprise by the Japanese at Pearl Harbor. But when did this happen?

3 Winston Churchill, whose quotes inspired Great Britain to victory again and again and as a result saved the world – no argument – became Prime Minister on which day?

4 The German invasion of France, you see, they started it, and if France were next door why would you invade? Who'd want that? The German invasion of France – mind you I suppose they did it 'cos the knew they'd win (and I'll thank all smartarses to pipe down, it was the French army collapsing on our right flank that meant we had to get out of there pronto – the Germans can't defeat you if you're not there) – started on which date?

5 D-Day was the day the Allies (and, whatever *Saving Private Ryan* might tell you, more British – and Canadian, respect due – troops landed on D-Day than Americans) stuck it to the Germans and the tide turned once and for all. But, what does the D in D-Day stand for?

Answers

1 3 September 1939. It was a Sunday. They started it, and ruined a weekend into the bargain. No wonder we had to defeat them.

2 7 December 1941. It was a Sunday, so the Americans were all washing their cars and playing Little League or something. What is Little League? No one knows. No one cares.

3 10 May 1940. It was a Friday. Typical British forward planning; get things in line for the weekend, so Monday morning you can hit the ground running.

4 10 May 1940. The very same day we got Winston. You win some, you lose some, eh? But a Friday – another weekend ruined by Hitler.

5 Day. The D stands for Day. That's the way the army likes to do things.

3 Science and Technology

(which might include a *Star Trek* question for the nerds)

We the British are the greatest scientific nation in the world. It goes without saying, though, whoops, there I said it. Isaac Newton was British and he thought up gravity, with nothing more than a garden and an apple tree to do it with. So, let's take a look at what you know about science and technology.

1 The British invented the computer, and they did it to crack the German codes and win the war. Another reason why you should be ashamed if you use the net for porn. But what was the name of the computer used at Bletchley Park?

2 We invented the railways. Fact. George Stephenson did it before writing *Treasure Island*. But what is the standard gauge for railways in this country, known also as the Stephenson gauge? Answers in metric not accepted.

3 Who invented the World Wide Web? As if he had in mind all the filth that followed. The nerd.

4 At what temperature does paper spontaneously combust? In Fahrenheit please, no metric measurements acceptable under any circumstances.

5 In *Star Trek* ... no actually, no. No, I won't do a *Star Trek* question. Sorry nerds. I said might. But I won't. What does a Geiger counter measure?

Answers

1 Colossus. They called it this because it was big. And by the time they'd invented the computer they were out of ideas.

2 4 feet 8 and a half inches. If you were that tall you'd be a midget.

3 Sir Tim Berners-Lee. The nerd.

4 842 °F. Not Fahrenheit 451. Sorry.

5 Radioactivity. You know, it makes that clicking sound. Of course, if it does make that clicking sound you're screwed. Thanks a lot, Professor Geiger.

4 Film and TV of the 1980s

1980s

TV and film was better in the 80s, that's what everyone who used to work in film and TV in the 80s says. And it was better, according to them, because they were working in it. Nod and say 'Yes, Grandad'. That's my advice. Have you ever seen *Juliet Bravo*? It's unwatchable. Anyway, let's crack on.

1 Ted Danson played TV's second-favourite barman* Sam Malone in the 1980s sitcom *Cheers*. A pub isn't a pub without its regulars (the same can be said too of the publican and the beer). Name two regulars who used to prop up his bar.

2 Possibly some of the worst films of the 1980s were the *Death Wish* films, made by director, restaurant critic and all round gastro-berk Michael Winner. How many of these God-awful films were made during the 1980s though?

3 Jim Robinson from *Neighbours* is now in *Lost*, *24*, *Ugly Betty*, *The O.C.* and *Indiana Jones and the Crystal Skull*. It's fair to say old Jim's come along since his days in Ramsay Street. Jason Donavan played his son in the Aussie soap, but what was the name of his character?

4 *Fraggle Rock* was made by Jim Henson, but featured fewer Muppets than most daytime car insurance adverts. Under which type of building did the Fraggles live?

5 Pierce Brosnan was the man who nearly broke Bond. Ouch. Thank God for the boy Craig. The thing is, Brosnan would have been Bond sooner, but he was contractually obliged to stink up television with a show in which he played the lead. What was it?

---

* Modesty forbids my saying who TV's favourite barman might be.

Answers

1 You could have chosen from Cliff Clavin, Norm Peterson and Frasier Crane.

2 Three. There were five in total in the series, but only three (in 1982, 1985 and 1987) were made during that particular decade. Listen to the question. Even Winner had had enough by *Death Wish III* and so left *Death Wish IV* and *V* to some other chancer.

3 Scott Robinson. It's fair to say Jason Donovan never made it to Hollywood. Or, to date, *Hollyoaks*.

4 A lighthouse. Though frankly in my view it could have been an outhouse.

5 *Remington Steele*. In which he played Remington Steele. It stank.

5 Pot Luck

Pot luck is basically what used to be called general knowledge, but since teachers decided knowing stuff was bad for us it can't be called that any more. Broken Britain! Get your thinking gear round this little lot.

1 Who wrote the Bangles' top-two hit (their only proper hit apart from *Walk Like an Egyp-shee-an* maybe, but that doesn't count 'cos it's daft), *Manic Monday*?

2 Animals now: pot luck, see? The Bangles one minute, animals the next. What kind of animals are Chester Whites, Hampshires and Durocs?

3 Rickets. Not had it myself but it's horrible apparently. Steve's nephew Alan had it. But which vitamin deficiency causes it?

4 Paddy Ashdown, remember him? Paddy Pantsdown, that was hilarious. What a bloke, he was a commando and a liberal. How does that work? Anyway: what is Paddy Ashdown's first name?

5 In the Bible – which is in English, never forget that, which makes it all the more remarkable given that it was written 2000 years ago in the Middle East by people who spoke Hebrew – what are the first five words of Psalm 23?

Answers

1 The pint-sized Prince of Pop, Prince. And that is his name, despite whatever half-arsed nonsense he might insist on.

2 They're pigs. Yes, pigs. Not chickens.

3 Vitamin D. Though God knows what that's in. Lager maybe.

4 Jeremy. Definitely a liberal.

5 'The Lord is my shepherd.'

6 Film and TV of the 1970s

Film and TV was better in the 70s, that's what everyone who used to work in film and TV in the 70s says. And it was better, according to them, because they were working in it. Nod and say 'Yes, Grandad'. That's my advice. Have you ever seen *Shoestring*? It's unwatchable. Anyway, let's crack on.

1 Al Pacino is famous for both mumbling and acting. He's been in many, many films such as *The Godfather*, *Scarface* and *Any Given Sunday* (although he doesn't like being reminded of that last one) but what did he have in Needle Park in 1971?

2 James Bolam was in the hit, I said hit, 1970s BBC sitcom *Whatever Happened to the Likely Lads*? He played Terry, the ex-army layabout. But which style of shoe did he sport throughout the entire series? I mean every episode. He wore them on every single show. What type of shoe was it?

3 *The A-Team* is looked upon nostalgically as a great piece of television, but having seen it re-run on Bravo recently, it's really not that good. In fact I'd like to break cover and say it was shit. What I would like to know is, according to the intro, in which year did the 'crack commando unit' get 'sent to prison by a military court for a crime that they didn't commit?'

4 *Doctor Who* is for children. And it's too vague. Not once does it tell you his surname and never does it specify what field he's specialised in. Although I'm guessing by how well he does with the ladies, looking at how fit his assistants are, he's more than likely a gynaecologist. But my question is: who was the longest serving Doctor Who? I mean who was the longest serving Doctor? Who? I mean who was the longest … Oh you get the idea. Who was it?

5 Ronnie Barker's *Porridge* showed a realistic portrayal of just how fun prison is. Ronnie of course played Norman Stanley Fletcher, and Lennie Godber was played by Richard Beckinsale. But which famous British writing duo wrote the series?

(Answers on page 20)

A Note on Mobile Phones etc, as in Bloody Cheating

Cheating is wrong. Cheating is bad. Cheating makes losers of us all. In Westerns they shoot you if you cheat at cards. The cheat puts the wrong cards down, bang goes a gun, the bloke falls out of his chair and spills precious cut-price firewater all over the shop. He has been dealt with, summary justice, the law of the frontier. Because cheats must never prosper.

But now, thanks to the mobile phone and the internet, cheating is everywhere. Cheating has become standard behaviour. And yes, the mobile has had an enormous – and some might argue improving – impact on relationships, what with sex texting, saucy pics etc, but the thing that is being undermined more than anything else is the Great British Pub Quiz. And let me tell it to you straight: the moment you pick up that mobile to try to get an answer, you are a villain, a heel, beyond the pale. You are letting yourself, your team, your pub, your county, your country, your people, your species down. Do you really want a frozen chicken you didn't honestly obtain? Unless it's the meat Irish Geoff brings in on Wednesday afternoons. And anyway, he did the dishonestly obtaining, you bought that chicken in good faith. Though personally I wouldn't risk it with one of Geoff's chickens, you need to go for the pork to be safe. But the fact remains that using a mobile phone to play a pub quiz is a crime up there with breaking and entering, GBH and treason. It is wrong and you know it is. End of. I can't think of an appropriate punishment that fits the crime, maybe we should cut your thumbs off.* Just because Tarrant lets you phone a friend doesn't mean you can. This isn't telly, this is real life. Grow up.

---

* Sorry to get all medieval on you there, but you have to have standards. Doesn't matter who you are, thumbs off. Side benefits? No more slap bass playing.

Answers

1 Panic. In a film called *Panic In Needle Park*. Panic is an obvious answer, it's the most likely thing you're going to have in a place called Needle Park. If anyone put 'a holiday' or 'a nice stroll' then you're clearly wrong and aren't even good at guessing. Leave now.

2 The desert boot. Seriously, he wore them in every episode, go back and check, apart from maybe the one where Bob got married. If you said brogues you've never seen it.

3 1972, or not soon enough clearly, having seen that show … And there was you thinking 'why was this in the seventies chapter?' Well now you know. You wouldn't be asking yourself that, had you known the answer.

4 Tom Baker.

5 Dick Clement and Ian La Frenais. I will accept Clement and La Frenais, but that's as far as it goes. I won't accept Galton and Simpson for this particular answer, although it might well be the correct answer to another question.

7 Space

1 It was Russian Yuri Gagarin who was the first man to make it into space, catching the Yanks out. They weren't expecting the Russians to beat them to it, mainly because they were being insufferably smug, as usual. But what was the date?

2 Who was the first American in space?

3 Who was the third man on the moon?

4 Famously, Neil Armstrong and Buzz Aldrin were the first men on the moon. But there was a third person who flew with them, but didn't actually get to go to the moon. What was his name?

5 What was the date of the first moon landing? And what day of the week was it for an extra mark.

Answers

1 12 April 1961.

2 Alan Shepard became the first American in space. An extra point if you can tell me the name of his spacecraft? It was *Freedom* 7. How did you know that? You really are a nerd, pal.

3 Pete Conrad. Ironically, old Pete made it to the moon and back in one piece but died in a horrific motorcycle accident. I don't know this for sure, but his last words may well have been 'Bollocks'.

4 Michael Collins. There was one unlucky bastard.

5 20 July 1969. It was a Sunday when they landed, and Monday when they got out. Some people think the moon landings were faked. I disagree; there's no way the Americans are clever enough to keep a lie like that going for so long, is there?

• •

What a diabolical decade. And before you argue, two words, well one word repeated, with which I make my case: Duran Duran. So bad they had to name it twice. Anyway, lots of other stuff happened back then. Here's some of it.

1 For most of the eighties the US President was Ronald Reagan, who charmed everyone by being old and doddery and saying he wanted to nuke Russia. Happy days. But who did he defeat to take office as President in 1981?

2 Band Aid – the band that changed the world, and resulted directly in Comic Relief every other year where a bunch of presenters who aren't comics try to bully us into coughing up again, even though the time before last they said they were going to Make Poverty History – all started when Bob Geldof wrote a record with who?

3 Live Aid, the concert that changed the world, blah blah blah blah blah blah blah blah blah blah blah Queen stole the show blah blah blah blah blah blah blah, took place in Wembley stadium in London and JFK Stadium in which American city?

4 Pat Cash once won Wimbledon. I know, it's amazing. So did Boris Becker, in 1985, when he was the first unseeded player, and the first German to win the men's singles. He was also the youngest player ever to win it. How old was he?

5 The Berlin Wall was a terrible thing, and a lasting legacy of the Second World War, but then they started it. But when did the Berlin Wall come down? Year and month please. An extra point if you can do the precise date.

Answers

1 Jimmy Carter, the peanut farmer.

2 Midge Ure. An extra point if you couldn't help yourself and said Midge Urine.

3 Philadelphia.

4 He was 17. But all you can think about is that broom cupboard.

5 9 November 1989.

9 British History

1 The Great Fire of London in 1666 is one of those events in history, like the Great War, that has been incorrectly named; there's nothing great about either of these two events and 'terrible' would surely be a more appropriate prefix. Anyway, in which lane did the Terrible Fire of London start?

2 Margaret Thatcher is the first and still the only female British Prime Minister in history, the housewife PM. They say, don't they, that if women ruled the world there would be fewer wars, which isn't strictly true as we were involved in our first major conflict for twenty-eight years under good old Maggie. What were the years of her reign?

3 The Battle of Hastings in 1066 is, for some reason known only to God, one of the first things we're taught at school even though it's the only time I can name that we lost to the French. What we should be doing is teaching all the little kiddies about the good stuff, like the Second World War, Vietnam and the Gulf parts 1 & 2. In which London setting was William crowned king of England?

4 Concorde no longer flies, because the French parts of the Anglo-French supersonic plane malfunctioned*, but in what year was its maiden flight?

5 I've only been on the railway once. It was overcrowded, stank of beer, fags, burgers and vomit and was at a complete standstill just outside the station for three hours. I've just realised that that was a pub called The Railway. I've never been on the railways, but between which two towns did the first public railway run?

---

* Of course they did.

Answers

1 It was started in Pudding Lane, by a total donut.

2 1979–1990. She's also blamed for causing massive unemployment during the 1980s, but she was actually only attempting to turn everyone into housewives, by getting rid of their jobs and making them stay at home.

3 Westminster Abbey.

4 1969. This was not a passenger flight. We took note from the Russians' early space missions and filled it with French people.

5 Darlington and Stockton. The first train left on 27 September 1825. This was way before the invention of excuses and therefore it had no choice but to arrive on time.

10 Numbers

Numbers – they rule our lives, according to that maths* teacher you never listened to. So, bow down before your lords and masters and answer these ...

1 Pi is one of the most important numbers ever figured out. It was the ancient Greeks who first came up with Pi, yet they didn't invent the pie itself, preferring kebabs, which are nowhere near as tasty (though a highly effective booze soaker, give credit where it's due). Pi is one of those numbers that goes on for ever: what is it to five places?

2 In the classic TV show from the 1960s called *The Prisoner* that only gets shown late at night to students, drunks, stoners and insomniacs, the hero was called Number 6. But who was his chief adversary?

3 How much did the new Wembley stadium cost when they finally finished the bloody thing? I won't ask how late it was, that's just embarrassing. Broken Britain!

4 Trafalgar Square commemorates the last time the French Navy did anything: sink. To commemorate it, the nation stuck Nelson on top of a giant telescope to look towards the scene of his greatest triumph. But how many lions are there in Trafalgar Square?

5 A prime number is the kind of number you can't divide, except by one and itself, so when you take a prime number of pounds on the till you have to trouser at least one to make it easier to cash up later in the evening. What are the first ten prime numbers?

---

* That's Maths, America, not Math.

Answers

1 3.14159. Right, get your breath back for the next one.

2 Number 2. Unfortunate name really.

3 £757 million pounds. That's right, £757 million. That's one pound per blade of grass on the pitch.

4 4. That's all, 4.

5 2, 3, 5, 7, 11, 13, 17, 23, 29, 31

11 Film and TV of the 1960s

Film and TV was better in the 60s, that's what everyone who used to work in film and TV in the 60s says. And it was better, according to them, because they were working in it. Nod and say 'Yes, Grandad.' That's my advice. Have you ever seen *Z Cars*? It's unwatchable. Anyway, let's crack on.

1 Everyone remembers *The Graduate*, you know, the film about the older woman and the younger man? He's a lucky boy, she knows what she's doing and above all she's grateful. Ben, the lad, was played by Dustin Hoffman, but who played Mrs Robinson?

2 Name the actress whose father was the original narrator of *The Magic Roundabout*.

3 *Hard Day's Night* was the first of the Beatles' films. Good job they brought out some decent records so they wouldn't be remembered for the movie careers alone. In which year was this film released?

4 Those of you old enough to remember the 1960s show *The Tales of Riverbank* will remember the acting being of a far superior quality to that seen on the much-missed show *The Bill*. Who narrated the British version of *Riverbank*?

5 Alfred Hitchcock's 1960 film *Psycho* is an undeniable classic[*]. It was at the forefront of film-making at the time and is still considered one of the top films ever made. Wouldn't it be a really pointless thing to do, to recreate it shot-for-shot but in colour, with none of the original cinematic magic? Name the director who pointlessly recreated it shot-for-shot but in colour, with none of the original cinematic magic?

---

[*] Though let's be honest, it's good but it's no *Zulu*. Goes on a bit in the middle.

Answers

1 Anne Bancroft. I've never had an experience with an older lady. In fact, it's been a long time since an experience of any sort with a woman of any age.

2 Emma Thompson. Her dad was Eric Thompson. *The Magic Roundabout* was originally a French show called *Le Manège Enchanté* (sounds like classic French filth to me). The British version is much, much better for obvious reasons, one of which being you can actually understand what they're saying.

3 1964.

4 Johnny Morris.

5 It was Gus Van Sant in 1998, who pointlessly recreated it shot for shot but in colour, with none of the original cinematic magic.

12 The Romans

The Romans, what a bunch they were. All more the unbelievable is the fact that they were Italian and conquered the world. How the hell did that happen? You have to be impressed in a way. Not that impressed though. Be reasonable.

1 Julius Caesar was the first Caesar. The clue is in the name, keep up. He was assassinated in the Senate – it says here – by all the other top Romans. What were reputed to be his last words?

2 The Romans wore togas and are therefore directly responsible for all the idiot frat-boy antics we have to put up with in American college movies. When they say it's a frat party at Delta Gamma Phi I just think, so bloody what? They also wore sandals, and they also liked baths. What was the name of the Roman Baths in Bath?

3 The Roman armies were feared all over the world, though they never defeated the Scots. Though understandably they built a wall to keep them out. How many men were in a typical Century?

4 Roman numbers are a nightmare, all those Ms and Xs and Vs and Ls and stuff. Not normal. The whole thing takes some working out. And now's your chance. How do you say 1984 in Roman numbers?

5 *Gladiator*, eh? What a film. Poor old Oliver Reed gasping his final between scenes and all that. Russell Crowe turns in a great one as the hero Maximus Decimus Meridius. How does he describe himself, and what does he vow?

Answers

1 'Et tu Brute'. 'And you Brutus'. At no point did anyone say 'Leave it Brutus, he's not worth it'.

2 Aquae Sulis.

3 83. The clue is not in the name.

4 MCMLXXXIV

5 'Father of a murdered son, husband to a murdered wife and I shall have my vengeance in this life or the next'. Why he didn't add 'outside now' remains a mystery.

13 Who's Who?

Calm down nerds, this isn't about Doctor Who. We're talking who's who. As in who is who. Not Doctor Who. Calm down. I'm asking you who certain people were, not who was Doctor Who. OK. So, who?

1 Who was known as Gregori Efimovich? That was his real name. But he was known as something else. It wasn't Doctor Who. Who was Gregori Efimovich?

2 Who is really called Harry Webb? That's his real name. But he's known as something else. What is it? It's not Doctor Who.

3 Who was dubbed 'the wisest fool in Christendom'? That wasn't his real name. It's what he ended up known as. Who was he? The wisest fool in Christendom?

4 George Eliot was a famous novelist, not that I've read anything by George Eliot. But apparently that wasn't George Eliot's real name. So who was George Eliot really?

5 Who (and we've managed a whole round of Who's Who questions without giving in to the temptation to do a Doctor Who question) was the original drummer in the Beatles?

Answers

1 Rasputin. Extra points if you wrote Ra-Ra-Rasputin.

2 Cliff Richard. Extra points if you wrote Cliff Ri-Ri-Richard. Unlikely I know.

3 James I. He was Scottish. Just saying.

4 Mary Ann Evans. That's right. A woman. What's that all about eh?

5 Pete Best. The first ever un-chirpy Scouser in the world. God that must hurt. Though mind you, he's probably not as grumpy as Ringo.

14 Film and TV of the 1990s

Film and TV was better in the 90s, that's what everyone who used to work in film and TV in the 90s says. And it was better, according to them, because they were working in it. Nod and say 'Yes, Grandad'. That's my advice. Have you ever seen *Party of Five*? It's unwatchable. Anyway, let's crack on.

1   *Baywatch* was watched by so many for totally the wrong reasons that they became the right reasons. That's my excuse and I'm sticking to it. David Hasselhoff was not a reason why anyone watched it, EVER*! But what was the name of his on-screen character?

2   *Noel's House Party* was a light entertainment show on the BBC during the 1990s, and it really was light on entertainment. Despite it being really very thin, it's endlessly plundered for ideas by the likes of Ant & Dec. What was name of the fictional village it was set in?

3   Barbara 'Babs' Windsor made men of boys when that bikini pinged off during *Carry On Camping*, but in which year did she start playing Peggy Mitchell in *EastEnders*? I've given you a fairly large clue by putting this question in the 1990s' section. You only have ten options to choose from.

4   The 1997 version of *Titanic* was too long, especially as you knew what was going to happen at the end. But even if you hadn't known, it was still too long. Despite this and it just not being that good overall, how many Oscars did it win?

5   True or false: 1999's *The Phantom Menace* was good?

---

* EVER!

Answers

1 Mitch Buchannon. I wouldn't blame you if you didn't get that right, no one will remember that, because it wasn't one of the bits in slow motion.

2 Hilariously, it was Crinkley Bottom, ha ha, Crinkley Bottom, that's priceless. The jokes that led to were just brilliant. Ha ha! Crinkley Bottom.

3 Ha ha, Crinkley Bottom, that's really funny. Sorry, the answer to the Barbara Windsor question is 1994. And that pinging bra. Come on.

4 How many? Sorry just read that for the first time. Eleven. Seriously I can't believe that. How on earth could that have beaten comedy of the year, *The Full Monty*?

5 False, it wasn't. No one liked it.

15 Sport: Mixed

Sport. Everyone loves it. Everyone. That doesn't include women, obviously. The ones who do sport are only doing it because their dads have bullied them into it in the hope they make millions.

1 In which year did the soft-core pornographic tabloid *Daily Sport* launch?

2 David Coulthard is responsible for the 'Coulthard Conundrum',* which is best described as: when he's winning he's British, but when he is losing he is very much Scottish. How many times in his fifteen seasons was he British? e.g. how many Grand Prix did he win?

3 Greg Rusedski is responsible for the 'Rusedski Paradox', which is best described as: when he's winning he's British, but when he is losing he is very much Canadian. He played twenty-seven singles finals in his career; how many times was he British?

4 The British invented cricket, as you will be aware. When we play other countries it's a test of their manners as to whether they let us win or not. Over the years, the Aussies have been very rude, but how many times have they beaten us at the Ashes before the 2009 series?

5 Peter Schmeichel used to be a goalkeeper for Denmark and Manchester United and helped them win titles including five Premier League titles, three FA Cup titles and the UEFA European Football Championship international title for Denmark. He is though more famous for his adverts on British television during the 1998 World Cup, but what product was he peddling? Clue: HE'S DANISH!

---

* See also the 'Murray Malaise' for tennis-playing cousin Andy.

Answers

1 1991. The morning dump hasn't been the same since.

2 13. Mainly Scottish then.

3 He won fifteen and was runner-up in twelve. Statistically, more British. I like Greg.

4 The Aussies have shown poor decorum on no less than thirty-one occasions. Rude bastards.

5 Danish bacon.

16 Guess the Lyrics

There are some people who can create images with words that can move you and there are some people who genuinely shouldn't be allowed to own a pen (sadly there is no law against this). The result: some truly awful lyrics. In this next round, I want both song and artist. You need both for a point.

1   *'I'm on a ride and I wanna get off but they won't slow down the roundabout/ I sold the Renoir and the TV set don't wanna be around when this gets out'*. This band not only sounds horrific, seeing it written down makes the blood curdle. Which band was it that was responsible for this lyrical atrocity against humankind and which song was it?

2   This next bloke (there's your first clue) hasn't quite grasped the structure of sentences in this feeble attempt, but this didn't stop him making more money than he had sense. *'Your butt is mine/ Gonna take you right/ Just show your face/ in broad daylight'*. Song and artist please.

3   *'I'm such a good good boy/ I just need a new toy/ I tell ya what girl/ Dance for me, I'll keep you over-employed'*. Which God-awful song are these lyrics from and which chancers sung them?

4   *'The line broke, the monkey get choke/ Burn bad rizzla upon him little rowing boat'*. Dear God, are we at the end of this round yet? Who sang this and what song was it?

5   *'Run around in circles, live a life of solitude 'till we find ourselves a partner someone to relate to/ Then we slow down, before we fall down'*. Not quite sure what this is all about, sounds a bit depressing, it's certainly no 'Bohemian Rhapsody' is it? That's not the question. The question is what is the song and who sang it?

Answers

1 The song was the Geordie anthem 'The Reflex' and the band was the toe-curlingly bad Duran Duran. I was going to ask how Simon Le* Bon sleeps at night, but annoyingly, it's next to Yasmin. How in God's name did that happen? Is there no justice?

2 The artist was Michael Jackson and the song was 'Bad'. No it really was, it was called 'Bad'. He was giving himself clues. We can all look forward to that being re-released endlessly now he's shuffled off.

3 This line is from the 1987 crime against music 'Girls, Girls, Girls' by the poodle-haired nonentities Mötley Crüe. No one would have heard of you lads, had your drummer not starred in that film with Pamela Anderson.

4 This is UB40 with their fruit-based hit for the ladies 'Red, Red Wine.' Frankly lads you should know better, rules is rules.

5 It was Robbie Williams singing his James Bond-riff-pilfering hit 'Millennium'. There should have been an expiry date on that song so it couldn't be played after midnight on 31 December 1999.

---

* French word.

17 Pot Luck

More random stuff.

1   In the French royal family (back when they had one, before they executed them because they didn't think it through and realise what a great tourist attraction they would become one day – idiots), what was the eldest son called?

2   Dolphins use echolocation to tell where they are. That's that horrible squeaking noise they make that people think is cute. Grow up. But in submarines, what is the echolocation thing called?

3   The Prince of Wales wrote a book once, and people were amazed. And rightly so. You wouldn't think he had it in him. No one's read it, not even him. What was it called?

4   When that was made into a film in America, they changed the title. They always do that, Yanks, for no other reason than they're stupid, and they can. What did they call the first Harry Potter film, which here was called *Harry Potter and the Philosopher's Stone*? (If you don't get this that's fine, it's for kids.)

5   Harry Potter star Daniel Radcliffe got out his todger, old fella, chap, little man, knob, schlong, piece, in a play recently. You have to respect me for resisting and not calling it a wand: but which play was it?

Answers

1 The Dauphin. Ours get to be Prince of Wales. Ouch. Though right now I don't know who's worse off in that deal. The Welsh or the Prince. Still, there's all those pubs named after him, free drinks for life.

2 Sonar.

3 *The Old Man of Lochnagar*.

4 They called it *Harry Potter and the Sorcerer's Stone* for no other reason than they're stupid and they could.

5 *Equus*, which is Latin for horse. Make your own stuff up here.

18 TV Chefs

There are almost as many TV chefs as there are hot dinners. You can't move for TV chefs these days. There they are on TV, cheffing, and not once do they point out that you've only got their word for it that the food's any good. Chancers.

1 Keith Floyd, God rest his really pickled soul, was my favourite of all the TV chefs and was a true publican's friend. What was the name of his first TV cookery show?

2 Bald, mad, scientific chef Heston Blumenthal would never get the gig as my chef in my pub and not because he's not a good bloke, but for one simple reason. I get frozen stuff (chips, sausages, burgers, peas etc) and cook them. He takes perfectly good food and freezes it using liquid nitrogen. You see, it would never work out – timewaster. He has his own place anyway so it's not as though he's short of cash. What is the name of his restaurant?

3 Nigella Lawson is by far the sauciest of all the TV chefs. I mean you would, wouldn't you? (Delia twenty years ago as well, yeah.) Her dad, Nigel Lawson, didn't stretch that far when choosing her name, but what position did he hold under the Thatcher government between 1983 and 1989?

4 TV chef Rick Stein, another publican's friend, by all accounts does a mean fish and chips. You just have to be bothered to go all the way to Cornwall to get it. For many years his little dog used to accompany him on his TV shows until he sadly passed a few years ago, but what was his name?

5 Which short-tempered, sweary and loud-mouthed TV chef's first autobiography was called *Humble Pie*?

Answers

1 *Floyd on the Floor, Floyd on the Night Bus, Floyd on the Sofa* and *Floyd on the Hair of the Dog at 9 a.m.*

2 It's called, not Heston Services, but the Fat Duck. Although it's not far from there, but to be honest when you're on the motorway you want a pork pie and crisps, not essence of sparrows' tears with peat compote. It was called the Frozen Duck, but it got left out in the sun.

3 He was Chancellor of the Exchequer. Six years of putting up the price of booze. He did give us Nigella, but still, you bastard.

4 Chalky. Listen Rick, don't despair, do what I did to my dog Ramrod and get him stuffed. Much cheaper to maintain and acts as a great doorstop in the summer months, don't you, boy?

5 Gordon Ramsay. And you know what? I take it back. Nowhere in that book was there a recipe for humble pie. Lots of stuff about how great he is, but not one recipe. Trading standards!

19 Kings and Queens

Royalty: we bow down before them because they are better than us, it is the natural order – after all, it's an animal kingdom not the Animal Socialist Worker's Republic. We have a long history of the best kings and queens in the world. What do you know about them?

1 You've got to have a mighty pair of bollocks to invent the role King of England and then give it to yourself, haven't you? Who claimed to be the first one?

2 Scotland had been asking to be part of England for years, so in the end we let them and in 1707 decided to call it Great Britain. Who was the first monarch of this great kingdom? I mean a united Britain? I mean … oh you know.

3 Has the US ever had a king?

4 The German Kaiser Wilhelm II is the bloke many think started the First World War, although there are some that say he was apprehensive. Yeah right, he was German, of course he was keen on a tear-up. He was related to the British monarchy at the time of the war, but how?

5 The current royal family are part of the House of Windsor (I've seen that place, it's a lot bigger than any house I've seen, classic royal modesty). The house before that was Saxe-Coburg-Gotha (Germans!) but what was the name of the house before that?

Answers

1 Offa of Mercia. Basically this Brummie fella decided that he was doing pretty well locally in Mercia (the Midlands) and he'd give himself the title Rex Anglorum. People didn't bat an eyelid, because they thought he was just saying he was Fisherman of Year. That was until some chap from Wessex came along who could speak Latin (not many public schools in them days), knew he was claiming to be King of England and told him to get on his bike. It's something like that anyway.

2 Anne of Great Britain. She got the job because of her name.

3 Yes, Elvis Presley. Again, self-appointed and often anointed.

4 He was the first cousin of King George V. And we complain when MPs hire their wives as secretaries!

5 House of Hanover (more Germans!). The house expected to supersede the House of Windsor is thought to be either the House of Beckhams or the House of Fraser.

20 Prime Ministers

It's the top job in the land. The job only the best and the brightest should aspire to. Oh well never mind. There's no dispute that Churchill was the best ever – if you disagree, leave now and return to the Fatherland – but there's been loads of 'em. What do you know?

1 There has to be a first of everything, even Prime Ministers. Which means that somewhere along the line it was decided that we actually needed one. Imagine that. Gawd. Who was the first Prime Minister?

2 We call them Prime Ministers, but they have another official title. Prime Ministers are called something else. What is it? Keep it clean.

3 How many Prime Ministers were there between Churchill and Thatcher? Not that any of the bastards count.

4 John Major eh? Hard to explain on any level really. Though a man prepared to fall on a grenade (e.g. Edwina Currie). He was Prime Minister for seven years, yeah, I know! But where was he MP for?

5 Between them, how many general elections did Margaret Thatcher (War Score: Falklands, on our own, no help from anyone else) and Tony Blair (War Score: multiple entries, some work in progress) win?

Answers

1 Sir Robert Walpole. Number One.

2 First Lord of the Treasury. They are also Minister for the Civil Service.

3 Nine, though Churchill had another go, and Wilson had two goes. But they count, that's how I'm counting it.

4 Huntingdon. They must have been so proud to start with.

5 Six. And how did their parties repay them? Proof if ever you needed it that MPs are a bunch of backstabbing bastards.

21 Food and Drink

Frankly I'm more interested in the latter, I'll be honest with you about that right now. After all, eating's cheating.

1 What makes up a proper ploughman's? This is a high-scoring question and there's a point for each correct ingredient.

2 This one is pretty thin, I'll admit, but stick with me. Name three musical acts that have fruit in their name?

3 Latte, espresso and cappuccino are all poncey versions of what drink?

4 Roald Dahl, Arlene Dahl and Sophie Dahl are all famous Dahls. But what is the main ingredient in the Indian dish dal?

5 Piers Morgan, Alan Carr and Deepak Chopra are all famous jerks (I don't use this word but it gives me a link for this question.) From which national cuisine does jerk chicken come from?

Answers

1 Mighty White not baguette; Cheddar not Brie; butter not marg'; pickle not chutney; and a piece of cucumber. No questions asked.

2 You could have had the Cranberries, Bananarama, Orange Juice, Dame Kiwi Te Kanawa, the Lemonheads, Black Grape, Blind Melon, Nicole and Natalie Appleton and Neneh Cherry, amongst others.

3 You should be too busy drinking tea to know this, so lose a point if you put coffee.

4 Lentils. Urgh, sounds disgusting. Not for me. That's what happens if you vote Liberal.

5 Caribbean. By the way, I've just realised I've left Jamie Oliver, Tom Cruise and Hitler off that list.

22 Pot Luck

1 Some people see a glass as half full, whilst others see it as half empty. This is said to be a good way of judging someone's character. I see a pint with half the amount in as someone drinking too slowly, and therefore I will be a judge of their character, thank you. But what is a quarter of a pint also known as?

2 Who invented the gas mask?

3 Who invented the corkscrew?

4 Who invented the internal combustion engine?

5 Who invented penicillin?

Answers

1 Noggin. You can't say that word any more, not since the race relations lads have clamped down.

2 The British, obviously. And we wouldn't have had to bother had the bloody Germans not invented poison gas.

3 The British, obviously. The French bang on about knowing their wine, but just think about this one, Jean Francois: had it not been for us, you wouldn't even know what it tastes like – you wouldn't have been able to get into the bloody bottle.

4 The British, obviously. It was never going to be the Aussies was it?

5 The British, obviously. To be more exact, it was Alexander Fleming, who found time to make the discovery in between writing Bond books.

23 The Romans

They built the Coliseum, they had straight roads, central heating under the floor, togas, spoke Latin, fed Christians to the lions and washed their teeth with piss. That's right. Piss. More questions on the Romans, coming up.

1   What were the names of the twins who supposedly founded Rome way back in the mists of time and who were suckled by a wolf? Disgusting. It's not like the Romans got off to a good start there. What does wolf milk taste like? That's not a quiz question. I'm just wondering, I don't want to know. No one does.

2   What was the Roman capital of Roman Britain when they settled here? I will not say conquered. We suckered them here so Boudica could give them a good kicking. That's my version of events and I'm sticking to it. What was the Roman capital of Roman Britain?

3   Augustus Caesar was the next Caesar after Julius Caesar (the clue's in the name, keep up) and was even his adopted son. What was he known as before he became Caesar?

4   In the film *Monty Python's The Life of Brian*, which as we all know brilliantly lampoons the foibles of organised religion with laser precision, what is the name of Pontius Pilate's friend who is visiting from Rome?

5   The Romans were renowned for all sorts of naughty behaviour and general lewdness. Which film-directing Roman has been on the run since 1978?

Answers

1 Romulus and Remus. Neither one of them was called Mowgli.

2 Colchester. What were they thinking? The A12 is murder on a Friday.

3 Octavian.

4 Biggus Dickus. Searing, incisive. That showed the Pope, the Archbishop of Canterbury, the Greek Orthodox Church, the Russian Orthodox Church etc etc.

5 Polanski.

24 Film and TV of the 2000s

Film and TV was better in the 2000s, that's what everyone who used to work in film and TV in the 2000s says. And it was better, according to them, because they were working in it. Nod and say 'Yes, kid'. That's my advice. Have you ever seen *Skins*? It's unwatchable. Anyway, let's crack on.

1 The film *Mamma Mia!* is a harrowing experience. People who can't sing singing, songs by Abba, a band who couldn't write a tune even if someone had written it for them. It's a film that makes a compelling case for suicide (not mine though). In which year did it come out?

2 *I'm A Celebrity … Get Me Out Of Here!* first aired in 2002 and ever since then there has been a God-awful stench in that air for about four weeks of the year. Tony Blackburn famously won the first series, but can you name three other celebrities, I mean contestants, from that first series?

3 Paul McGann unfortunately failed to kill off Doctor Who once and for all in a made-for-TV movie in 1996. It returned in 2005 and its saving grace was that Billie Piper was on our screens every week, playing the Doctor's assistant. What was the full name of her character? By full name I mean I want her surname too, donut.

4 The *Lord of the Rings* films were not only for kids, nerds and the friendless, but were also some of the most successful movies of the 2000s (notice I didn't say noughties, that's because I don't write for *Heat* magazine). Which of the trilogy was the only one not to be the highest grossing film in its year of release?

5 *EastEnders* is the best sitcom on British television, no question, conversation over. During the 2000s two characters appeared that made the show even more laughable. Alfie and Kat, the great lovers of the square. Alfie Moon was of course played by Shane 'The Legend' Richie (Bobby Ball, of Cannon and Ball fame, apparently gave him this nickname, seriously), but who played Kat Slater?

(Answers on page 58)

Star Trek: Why is It Always in Quizzes?

Space, the final frontier. With these immortal words history was made, and mankind set course on its new future, as a subspecies of human was brought into being. According to Charles Darwin's evolution theory thing, a separate species comes into being when the circumstances of the environment change and then cause changes (roughly). *Star Trek*'s arrival changed circumstances by providing a new kind of TV for young minds to feed on – sci-fi – and then caused changes, bringing into being a new species. And this separate species were nerds. Soon, it is reckoned – by me mainly, though some of the lads in the pub agree with this too – nerds will become so separate from other humans that they will be unable to breed with normal *homo sapiens* (though to be honest, this might be because normal *homo sapiens* don't want to breed with them, urgh).

Even as Kirk stared into the middle distance to bark his choice of philosophical blather to no one in particular, humanity began to change. Now, four thousand episodes of *Trek* later (roughly, I haven't checked that one) the nerd hive has taken over telly; being a nerd has almost become respectable, especially now that computers are everywhere. I've never been online for anything other than what the internet was intended for – eh, gents? But nerds use it to make friends with each other (otherwise impossible for them), talk about *Star Trek*, swap *Star Trek* pictures, organise *Star Trek* parties, quibble over *Star Trek* continuity ... Is this what computer-inventing gay* bloke Alan Turing had in mind when he invented the computer? I think not. But there it is. It does make you hope that we colonise space soon, because the people who are going to volunteer to go will be the nerds and then we can be spared the embarrassment of relying on them to help when the

---

* I am being homofactual by mentioning that.

server goes down. But the reason it's always in quizzes is this: for while *Star Trek* may have been a cataclysmic event in the history of humankind on a par with leaving our Neanderthal cousins for dust, it is also a sci-fi show everyone has seen a bit of. So you stick it in a quiz rather than *Battlestar Galactica* or *Stargate: Universe*. And in case you were wondering, *Doctor Who* is different, that's British and therefore normal.

Answers to Round 24

1   2008. Can we move on to the next question? I don't want to think about this anymore.

2   You could have chosen from Tara Para Tinkleplink, Christine *'you know, I'm Neil's wife'* Hamilton, Nell McAndrew, Rhona Cameron, Darren *'I sleep in my car'* Day, Nigel Benn and Yuri *'Do you need me to talk about Michael Jackson yet?'* Geller. Can we move on to the next question? I don't want to think about this anymore.

3   Rose Tyler. Not sure what's more unbelievable, the TARDIS (bigger on the inside etc) and time travel, or that Billie Piper was once married to Chris Evans.

4   *The Fellowship of the Ring*, which got beaten by *Harry Potter and the Philosopher's Stone*. It seems the kids, nerds and friendless had a lot to choose from that year.

5   Jessie Wallace. I've lost the will to live, what's the next topic?

25 Colours

What's your favourite colour? Well I won't be asking that, obviously, that would be a waste of time, wouldn't it?

1   Walkers crisps are the best, end of story. I'm not just saying that because I appeared in one of their commercials, no, but because they are the best. Mmmm, ready salted. What colour is a bag of Walkers cheese and onion crisps?

2   In the visual spectrum, which colour is of a number of similar colours evoked by light consisting predominantly of the longest wavelengths of light discernible by the human eye, in the wavelength range of roughly 630–740 nanometres?

3   It starred Whoopi Goldberg, Danny Glover and Oprah Winfrey, was nominated for eleven Oscars but didn't win any. What colour was it?

4   It has three horizontal stripes, from the top: black, red and gold. I wish I could say it was a multipack of Walkers crisps, but it isn't. What is it?

5   There are loads of colours with stupid names that seem to have been invented by paint companies and interior designers to humiliate men and bamboozle women, and set newlyweds against each other. Taupe is one of them. Cyan is another. What colour is cyan?

Answers

1 It's blue. And for some reason salt and vinegar is green.
   No one can explain that. It's so obviously wrong. That's
   the only thing I'd change about Walkers crisps.

2 It's red. The colour of ready salted. The best flavour.

3 Purple. Worcester sauce flavour. All wrong. Worcester
   sauce is for putting into baked beans, not licking off
   crisps.

4 The German flag. They've been too quiet for too long.
   If you see that one coming towards you, it's on again!

5 Cyan is a bluey green. If you got that right and you're not
   a paint manufacturer or interior designer, ask yourself
   how you know.

26 World War Two Dates

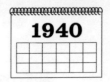
1940

I don't know how you did on the last lot of dates: my guess is the older folks amongst you knew this stuff in your sleep, whereas the youngsters among you didn't know any of it, seeing as you can get an A-level in History just by putting your date of birth on top of the paper. So here we go again.

1 At the end of the last round of questions about World War Two dates, I asked you what the D in D Day stood for and some of you might have got that right, while the rest of you would have been relieved that I didn't ask what the date was. But we're back on World War Two dates now, so pay attention and tell me this: what date was D Day?

2 The Germans surrendered – having lost the war, and fair enough, they started it – but the Allies had to agree on a day for the war ending. What date was VE Day?

3 The plot to kill Hitler, which had nothing whatsoever to do with Tom Cruise, no matter what the movies might have you believe, reached its moment of abject stupid failure when they failed to blow him up on what date?

4 The first atom bomb was dropped on Hiroshima by the Americans, a terrible historic event that changed the world for ever. Though it meant the Japanese began to reconsider the folly of taking on America and her mighty allies; after all, it was British scientists who developed the atom bomb, but we got the Americans to build and test it in their country. But on what date did this occur?

5 The Japanese surrendered pretty shortly after that – even though one or two of them carried on on Godforsaken islands awaiting orders from the Emperor right into the 1970s. What date did Emperor Hirohito call it a day?

Answers

1 6 June 1944. It was a Tuesday. We weren't going to ruin anyone's weekend, not even Hitler's. An essential difference between democracy and Nazism.

2 8 May 1945. It was a Tuesday. Plenty of time to clear the place up in time for the weekend. Magnanimous in victory.

3 20 July 1944. A Thursday. Obviously the plotters wanted to get the war over with before the weekend.

4 6 August 1945. It was a Monday. That way the Japanese had all week to reconsider.

5 15 August 1945. A Wednesday. And you know what? A lot of people give up on stuff midweek; it seems even the Japanese are no exception.

27 Disney Films

Walt Disney amazingly made his fortune out of that God-awful annoying mouse. In America, they all love the mouse as if it's really good, when in fact it seems to me that the mouse has pretty much no redeeming qualities at all*. That duck's not much better. As for the dog ... Well, there's two dogs. Once you've seen *Tom and Jerry* there's no going back. But, anyone with kids has watched most Disney films a minimum of four hundred times (well it beats playing with them, God, toddlers are tedious).

1 In the film *The Little Mermaid* with the somewhat dodgy West Indian accented lobster – 'Under der sea, under der sea...' – what is the name of the mermaid?

2 *Pinocchio* is the heartwarming tale of a wooden puppet who wants to ... sorry, nodded off there. I'll try again: *Pinocchio* is the heartwarming tale of the wooden puppet who wants to become a real boy. It's twee, at best. What is the toymaker's name?

3 *Snow White* was the first full length Disney feature film but I will not ask you to name the seven dwarves, there's no point. Which year was it released?

4 Everyone loves *The Jungle Book*, though the best bits are 'The Bare Necessities' and the 'I wanna be like you' bit. You have to just sit through the rest and grin and bear it pretty much. Who are the vultures excruciatingly modelled on?

5 Tarzan – raised by apes. Yuk. What is ape milk like? I don't know, and I don't want to know. Whoever thought that up is a sick, sick man. Disney made a Tarzan film in 1999 – who won an Oscar for the film's theme song?

---

* It's an opinion.

Answers

1 Ariel. That lobster is bang out of order. The world's changed mate.

2 Geppetto.

3 December 1937 was the premiere. It went into full release in February 1938. So I'll accept either.

4 The Beatles. It's terrible, truly God-awful. Is that what John Lennon died for?

5 British hitmaker Phil Collins.

28 Who's Who?

OK, more of the who questions. Not Doctor Who. Questions about who certain people might be. Not about Doctor Who. How many times? Knock it off, will ya?

1 David Bowie had a hit with Queen with the single 'Under Pressure' – which no one can deny was the best thing he ever did. In fact, it's fair to say that with 'Under Pressure' Bowie achieved classic status. But all this time he's been living a lie – he's not really called David Bowie. What's his real name?

2 Who are the House of Saxe-Coburg-Gotha?

3 A rose by any other name would smell as sweet, someone said, though I think if it was called a Dungshitflower you might dispute that*, but lots of bands have taken their time deciding what to call themselves. The Beatles were called the Quarrymen, then the Silver Beatles; Radiohead were called On A Friday; Queen were called Smile; who were the High Numbers?

4 The next one is what's called a *nom de plume*. Trust the French to have a word for calling yourself something else so you can deny the rude things you wrote about someone. Who was Samuel Langhorne Clemens? Mind you, you might change it if that was your name.

5 The Germans have lost a couple of wars – but they started them, never forget, and if you can't stand the heat get out of the kitchen. But on both occasions they put up one hell of a fight. One who was part of them was the Red Baron, but what was his name?

---

* Shakespeare: he didn't think it through. But then, that doesn't surprise you does it?

Answers

1 David Jones. David Jones and Queen. Not got the same ring has it? But with Queen involved it would be a hit whatever he was calling himself.

2 The royal family. If that doesn't tell you they're Germans, nothing will.

3 The Who. Come on, the clue's in the name of the round.

4 Mark Twain. Good call.

5 Manfred Von Richthofen. They still lost though.

29 Compulsory Literary Round

My publisher told me I needed a round on books and what have you, so here we are. I don't read books, except my own of course (but I have to – it's hard not to read it while you're writing it. In fact it would be impossible unless you had your eyes closed.)

1 The Japanese, it's fair to say, like the simple life; they don't cook their fish, they can't be bothered with proper cutlery and don't even have laces in their shoes. So you can imagine how little effort they put into their poetry. How many lines in a Japanese haiku poem?

2 The English dictionary is by far and away the best dictionary in the world. Of course it is, it's easier to read than the other ones. You don't need a dictionary to read it. Not like French books. Which author is credited with creating the first proper and reliable English dictionary?

3 The *Lord Of The Rings* films did so well that they made them into books. J. R. R. Tolkien wrote them, that's easy, so I'm not going to ask you that question. What I want to know is, what does the J. R. R. in J. R. R. Tolkien stand for?

4 Unbelievably, Jordan's Wikipedia page lists her as being 'Actress, author, businesswoman, media personality, philanthropist, glamour model, producer, singer, songwriter and television personality'. The most unbelievable of all of these is 'author.' Come on love, who are you kidding? What is the name of the first novel that Jordan supposedly wrote?

5 Mad old Mark Chapman made his name by shooting John Lennon. Time waster. He was supposedly obsessed by *The Catcher In The Rye*, which he said drove him to it. Who wrote that book?

Answers

1 Three. Come on lads, you can do better than that. Apparently this is the best-known haiku ...

> old pond ...
> a frog leaps in
> water's sound

Really? OK, here's one for you.

> My beer ...
> I like my beer
> My beer good

2 Doctor Samuel Johnson. Top bloke.

3 John Ronald Reuel. A bonus if you know what the J.R. in J.R from Dallas stands for.

ANSWER John Ross.

And for one final bonus point, what does the J. R. stand for in J. R. Hartley?

ANSWER He doesn't exist, grow up. Lose a point for even attempting to answer this.

4 *Angel*. Apparently this book is about a woman who becomes a model. Jesus Christ ...

5 J.D. Salinger. So really in a way it's his fault. Nice one Jerome.

30 Famous Quotes – Philosophers   66...99

Philosophy – what's the point, eh? Not that they ever ask themselves that question. If you're so brainy why don't you get on with curing the common cold or something?

1 *'Education is the best provision for old age.'* No, I think you'll find a decent care home is your best provision. Don't expect them to care once you're no use to them. And an education won't help you get to the remote in the TV room first. It's not education you need my friend, it's a decent bloody wheelchair. Who said this insensible nonsense?

2 *'Men are born ignorant, not stupid. They are made stupid by education.'* Hear, hear, that's more like it. This bloke has to be British. This is precisely the reason my old man didn't send me to school. He's said nothing about working in a pub making you stupid, has he? The question is, who said it?

3 *'I would believe only in a God that knows how to dance.'* This has got to be one of those chancers off that Pineapple Studio show. Who said this?

4 Who said this: *'Landlords, like all other men, love to reap where they never sowed'*? Clearly someone who doesn't know the pub trade. It's almost impossible to make a living nowadays. Even the blokes with carveries are suffering.

5 Who uttered this nugget of wisely wisdom: *'Touch my bum, this is life'*?

Answers

1 Aristotle. What a chancer, I'm guessing he died alone, not able to fix the gears on his Stannah stairlift. So much for your education, pal.

2 Bertrand Russell. I bloody knew it! The only half-decent bit of philosophising and it's by a British bloke.

3 Friedrich Nietzsche. German, 'nuff said.

4 It was Karl Marx. Another German. You can't trust this bloke. This is the bloke who said 'I am not a Marxist', which is a bit like Hitler saying 'I am not an arsehole' really isn't it?

   ANSWER Yes.

5 This was in fact the Cheeky Girls. Very existential I think you'll agree. Mind you, you can always tell what a girl's going to look like by taking a look at her mother. Oof.

31 Kings and Queens

I love the royals, and would happily punch in the face of anyone who disagrees with me. What Harry and Wills and Charles need to know is I've got their backs, no questions asked. If Harry wants to come to my gaff and let his hair down, he's welcome any time. Especially if he's prepared to spend eight grand a pop on bubbly that everyone knows is £4.75 at the cash and carry.

1 Kings sometimes pick up nicknames along the way, and sometimes they give you a good clue about what they were really like. Which king was known as the Sailor King?

2 Billy Connolly once cropped up in a film where he had to fall in love with Queen Victoria, played by Judi Dench. *That's* acting. What was the name of the film?

3 King Edward VII was king after Queen Victoria; he hung around his whole life waiting for his mum to shuffle off, which must have made Christmas a lot of fun. He spent a lot of that time in whorehouses in Paris, the filthy royal bastard. But his first name wasn't Edward. What was it?

4 Sometimes kings and queens take proper wrong turns and do things they really shouldn't. Which queen was married to Phillip II of Spain?

5 Which king got himself into a proper mess and ended up known as Lackland?

Answers

1 William IV. David Cameron is a descendant of one of William IV's bastard offspring. That's how posh he is.

2 *Mrs Brown.*

3 Albert, after his dad, Prince Albert, who is no relation to the Prince Albert.

4 Mary I. What was she thinking?

5 King John. What kind of nickname is that? Makes you wonder what Wills is going for. The Chinook Prince?

32 Pot Luck

1 Who is sixth in line to the throne? And I'm not talking about the queue for the gents.

2 Which film, in the author's opinion, is the worst movie of the 1970s, by a very long margin?

3 Which airline is based out of Dubai? They have the best uniform, oof, though the Qantas girls look good too. If only I had a passport and hadn't lost it in the last fire for insurance and tax purposes.

4 The Monkees. 'Hey hey we're the Monkees' they used to sing and you'd love the theme tune and the titles when they walked all over the place with a surfboard and all that, and then gradually you'd realise that the show itself was pretty dull. One of them was British, too. However, Mike Nesmith's (one of the tall ones) mum invented what?

5 One of the other Monkees, the one who looked like he was playing the drums, but maybe wasn't*, was called Mickey Dolenz. He came up with which hit 1980s kids TV show that some out-of-ideas berk is bound to copy sooner or later?

---

* Legendary American session drummer Hal Blaine did most of their stuff.

Answers

1 Princess Eugenie of York. Hmmm, doesn't fill you with much confidence does it, that fact? And you look at who's before her, Christ. Princess Beatrice of York (yeah exactly, me neither.) Prince Andrew (anything that moves, that man.) Prince Harry. (The Ginger Ninja). Prince William (what is it about that bloke, one minute he looks like his mum, the next minute he looks like a balding horse?) And finally Prince Charles, who really, all things considered, is the only sensible one out of the lot of them.

2 It's *Grease*, which, as anyone sensible will tell you, is diabolical. Give yourself an extra point if you agree with me.

3 Emirates.

4 Liquid Paper. That stuff for when you make a mistake typing. Like what word-processing made obsolete. Mind you, I'm dictating this into a tape recorder, how it gets typed up is none of my business.

5 Metal Mickey. His catchphrase was 'Metal Mickey'. Simpler times.

33 TV Chefs

They're everywhere I tells yer! TV chefs! You can't move for the bastards, telling us how to eat and what to eat and then purely by coincidence appearing in ads for supermarkets.

1 Delia Smith broke the mould of TV cookery, with her down-to-earth approach to making the business of dead-ahead simple cooking accessible to everyone, but now she is best known for getting drunk at the football. Which football club is it? Nice pies there you know.

2 He rides a scooter, and he is without a doubt a bloody great bloke. He went to Italy in a camper van, whoopy bloody do. But what did Jamie Oliver charge at his restaurant Fifteen for beans on toast or, as the pukka mucker called it, Best Baked Bean Bruschetta?

3 Gary Rhodes – he has spiky hair, that's his gimmick – was one of the chefs on *Hell's Kitchen*, ITV's answer to the question 'What's on after *The Bill*'? Who was his opposite number in the other kitchen, not sure if it was the red or the blue, not like it matters, eh?

4 Hugh Fearnley-Whittingstall, Britain's premier river cottager, cuts up pigs and cows and chickens, laughing and crying at the same time because they are his friends yet he must eat them. But he's not just someone who loves killing animals on telly, he's a fully trained chef. Where did he start out?

5 Ainsley Harriott – he always ends up doing the washing up in the ads, he needs to have a word with his agent – before he got his break as a TV chef was in a double act. What was it called?

---

* RIP.

Answers

1 Norwich City.

2 Seven quid. Can you believe it? Chancer.

3 Jean-Christophe Novelli. Who has been here two decades so ought to be able to pronounce words ending in '-tion' properly and not like Inspector bloody Clouseau.

4 The River Café. So did Jamie. They seem to specialise in really great blokes*.

5 The Calypso Twins. Don't panic, there aren't two of him.

---

* Sometimes it just doesn't come across on the page.

34 Guess the Lyrics

It can't be easy coming up with words for pop songs, and there are loads of top pop stars who prove again and again how hard it truly is. Some of these are woeful, and if you gave up the will to quiz I'd understand completely.

1 *'Reach up for the sunrise/ Put your hands into the big sky/ You can touch the sunrise/ Feel the new day enter your life.'* Who on earth wrote these? Well, I say wrote, if you did write these down and then read them back to yourself, you'd say 'nah' and go back to hanging around the dole office or whatever fate had in store for you.

2 These words might well be the ones that send you over the brink: *'Yesterday was easy/ Happiness came and went/ I got the movie script/ But I don't know what it meant'*. It can't be easy getting through a second verse back to the chorus, but this hardly does the job, does it? What's it from?

3 *'Soft and cuddle hug me up like a quilt/ I'm a lyrical lover no take me for no filth/ With my sexual physique Jah know me well built/ Oh me oh my well well can't you tell/ I'm just like a turtle crawling out of my shell'*. Who on earth said that lot?

4 OK, listen to this. None of it rhymes, but they think you won't notice because if you did you'd crash the car in an effort to destroy your car radio. *'I could stay awake just to hear you breathing/ Watch you smile while you are sleeping/ While you're far away dreaming'*. Who's this then?

5 And finally in this round, who came up with this farrago of nonsense, bearing in mind that by the time they wrote it they were multimillionaires? *'This is for the ones who* *stood their ground/ For Tommy and Gina who never backed down'.*

(Answers on page 80)

Here's some space to rest your beer . . .

Keeping Score

Keeping score is what the pub quiz is all about. You want to score more than the other teams, dead simple. The team with the most points wins. Waltzes off triumphant in the knowledge that their knowledge is bigger than everyone else's. But there is a second type of score-keeping in operation in a pub quiz: the internal team score-keeping, the needle, the long lingering grudges, the power struggles for supremacy within the team. If someone has a round that goes well – usually the movie round – it's only human of them to remind the others of their indispensability to the team. Over and over again. If they've had a beer maybe they will become like the proverbial dog with the proverbial bone and not let it drop all night. Certainly at next week's quiz they will bring it with them and wear their movie-round prowess like a gaudy medal. But in the pub-quiz world, fate is a fickle mistress and all too easily a team member's supremacy can be whipped away from them by a series of questions about 1960s movies that they simply know no answers to. Then the bile of recrimination can overwhelm and distract the team through the next couple of rounds – the sour mantra of defeat ('you said you knew movies!') blocking out the question master's measured tones, and their game descends into confusion and defeat. I can offer no advice as to how to combat this all-too-understandable potential in every team for losing its balance in this way – after all, if someone does well you want them to enjoy the moment. But the best pub quiz teams are the ones who don't utter a word all evening, who are concentrated, focused, poised. They maybe exchange terse glances, raised eyebrows, muttered replies. They don't look like they're having fun, and there's a reason for that: they're not having fun, they're winning. Don't forget, when Tiger Woods started having fun it coincided with him losing. No one said it was easy – no one ever said it would be this hard.

Answers

1 Duran Duran with (*Reach Up*) *For the Sunrise*. Them
  again. Sometimes, when I need to stay awake, like in the
  car, I get to thinking about Simon Le Bon's* uncommon
  run of luck, and my blood boils with such fury, envy and
  jealousy that I have no problem for the rest of the
  long journey.

2 Razorlight's hit let 'America'. Bloody hell. You know he's
  gone on record saying their debut album was better than
  Bob Dylan's. Donut.

3 Shaggy, with his hit 'Boombastic'. And if that's his
  opening chat-up line he's got a lot of work to do.
  Everyone knows the most reliable opening gambit is
  'I like your hair'. It's amazing what people like, isn't it?

4 Aerosmith, with their power ballad 'I Don't Want to Miss
  a Thing'. One word: toilet.

5 Bon Jovi, 'It's My Life'. If ever you need to understand the
  difference between Great Britain and America, look at it
  like this. They got Bon Jovi, we got Queen. I rest my case.

---

* French word

35 Famous Daves

Dave

Everyone knows a Dave. Daves are one of the crucial constituent particles that make up this great country of ours. Throughout our history there have been Daves who have made a difference at the crucial moment, starting off with Dave Number One, the original and best, Dave who lamped old Goliath. So, time to test your Dave knowledge with some questions of Dave.

1   Daves are so important to the fabric of the world, they've even got their own TV channel. What did it used to be called before it was called Dave?

2   In the film *Dave*, which is about a bloke called Dave, who, thanks to a mix-up, ends up being the President of the USA even though he's just a bloke called Dave, who plays Dave?

3   Wake up your team geek, he'll know this one: which Dave played Doctor Who?

4   Which Dave was overtaken by Mika Häkkinen with two laps remaining of the Australian Grand Prix in 1998?

5   Whose locker is at the bottom of the sea?

Answers

1 UKTV G2. Which doesn't spell Dave.

2 Kevin Kline plays Dave. Why they didn't just get a bloke called Dave I don't know. It's not like there's a shortage of Daves.

3 Dave Tennant. The D in TARDIS stands for Dave. Everyone knows that.

4 Dave Coulthard. He was leading but they had an agreement that whoever had got to the first corner first got to win the race. At least that was Dave's story and he was sticking to it.

5 Dave Jones. Not Davey. Famous Daves. That's the name of the round.

36 Food and Drink

(second helpings, ha ha ha ha ha ha)

1 The Irish, as we know, love the craic, but they don't love
   the craic as much as they like the Guinness; in fact some
   say the craic is totally dependent on whether there is
   Guinness involved. It's a strange drink that looks and
   tastes a bit like liquidised burnt toast, yet you are able
   to have ten in a row in a way that you couldn't with ten
   slices of burnt toast. What is the alcohol content of
   liquidised burnt toast, I mean Guinness?

2 Sushi, of course, isn't real food and was in fact invented
   in the Japanese prisoner of war camps during the Second
   World War as punishment for not obeying orders. But
   what does the word literally mean?

3 The Polish are famous for their hard graft, excellent use
   of power tools and for getting jobs done quicker and for
   half the price. On Polish cuisine, what is borscht?

4 The Victorians were known for being innovative and
   clever. However, anyone who designs a house and puts
   the toilet a hundred feet down the garden doesn't get my
   vote. They also used to eat some really disgusting food.
   One such dish is kedgeree, which is rice with fish and
   curry powder – sounds like a horrible mix of leftovers –
   and worst of all they ate it for breakfast. Do you know
   what type of fish is used in kedgeree?

5 I never have and never will make or serve cocktails in
   my pub. It's never going to happen. Cocktails are drunk
   by Mini-driving estate agents who call everyone 'dude'
   and holiday in places far too hot to enjoy. Cocktails have
   stupid names designed to embarrass the people ordering
   them and the poor bloke who has to make them, and
   once ordered are the source of much hilarity with names
   such as 'Sex on the Beach' and 'Barking Spider'. What
   ingredients go into the Tom Collins cocktail?

Answers

1 Don't drink the stuff myself but I know the answer is 4.1%. I will however accept 4.2% as I'm feeling generous.

2 Strangely it doesn't mean 'lazy', 'not cooked' or 'overpriced' but does in fact mean 'vinegared' or 'sour.'

3 It's beetroot soup. Christ, with food like that no wonder they are so keen to get back to work.

4 It's smoked haddock. Can you imagine going into the office smelling of that?

5 Gin, lemon juice, sugar, and carbonated water. Sounds horrible. Not that I'd ever try one. Not normal.

37 Formula 1

Formula 1 is the best sport of them all. By miles. You can lie on your couch watching it and experience the thrills and spills of twenty or so other blokes miles away in a luxury location having more excitement in an hour and forty five minutes than you will in an entire lifetime, then going on back to the hotel and having even more fun while you leave the telly on for *Antiques Roadshow*.

1 Altogether now: Dum, dumdy dum, dumdy dumdy dum dum. When was the first official Formula 1 season held?

2 Juan Manuel Fangio was widely regarded as the greatest driver of all time, winning the world championship five times, in 1951, 1954, 1955, 1956 and 1957. Sounds to me like he was too keen. It wasn't till Schumacher came along that his record was beaten. But where was he from? (Not Schumacher, we all know that).

3 Niki Lauda, hard as nails, got back in his car how many weeks after it burst into flames at the Nurburgring? Not the same car obviously, that would have been really stupid.

4 Damon Hill, World Champion in 1996, drove that season for Williams. It was beautiful, he saw off Schumacher and everything. Who did he drive for next?

5 How many Grands Prix had Jenson Button started when he won at the Hungarian Grand Prix in 2006? Clue: it's loads. Loads and loads.

Answers

1 1950. Before Fleetwood Mac wrote the music for it. They didn't think it through.

2 He was from Argentina.

3 A mere six weeks. Nails.

4 TWR Arrows. Though I will accept Arrows. To be honest, most Hill fans have erased it from their memories.

5 113. Slowly slowly catchee monkey.

38 Famous Steves

I've already done a famous Daves round, and so there's no fights in the pub when the book comes out, I'll do a famous Steves round. You have to treat the Steves and Daves as equals if you want things to run smoothly, trust me.

1 Steve Wonder has spanned decades singing and playing the piano much better than half those oiks out there who have had the head start of actually being able to see the keyboard. They don't make them like him any more. He wasn't born with either sight or the name Steve Wonder, so what is his legal name?

2 Liverpool and England ball-kicking maestro Steve Gerrard recently said his favourite type of cheese was what?

3 Which famous Steve wrote *A Brief History Of Time*?

4 Saint Steve (or just plain old Steve as he was known back then) was brutally stoned to death for blasphemy against Moses (I think he laughed at his sandals) and was later canonised, which is as pointless as being inducted into the Rock and Roll Hall of Fame after you've snuffed it. We celebrate St. Steve's day every year, but what do we more commonly know it as?

5 Who is the famous Steve who is known for making straight-to-video films such as *Under Siege*?

Answers

1 Steveland* Morris.

2 'Melted.' I'd have to say mine is grated. But then, as a footballer, he's a man in a hurry and probably hasn't got the time to grate as well as melt.

3 Steve Hawking. I had a go at that book, it was 240 pages! He has a very funny idea of the word 'brief'. Chancer. Still, good luck to him.

4 Boxing Day. Although, these days they mostly show football.

5 Steve Seagal. He's made some truly dire films and yet people still claim to like him in that really annoying 'it's so bad, it's good' ironic way. Grow up everyone involved.

---

* That is his name, I've checked.

39 World War Champions of the World

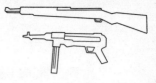

This round isn't really a set of pub quiz questions, it's me trying to make a point. Great Britain is world war champion of the world, heavyweight, now medium/bantamweight. So here's some questions to make it perfectly clear who's the daddy at world war.

1 Who won World War One?

2 Who started it?

3 Who won World War Two?

4 Who started it?

5 There isn't a fifth question here really.

Answers

1 We did.

2 They did.

3 We did.

4 They did.

40 Sport: Tennis

1 There have been some great nicknames in tennis over the years; Pistol Pete, The Federer Express and Andy 'Hot Rod' Roddick. Yet when it comes to the British players these nicknames go all limp like old lettuce. Tiger Tim just sounds ironical and Grinning Greg just makes him sound like his shorts are too tight. We can't let this happen to Andy Murray; he needs a decent nickname. Only one point available to the whole room here and it goes to the team that comes up with the best nickname for Andy Murray.

2 Wimbledon is the best tennis tournament in the world, no question. One of the reasons being it's the easiest one to get to. What are the first four characters of the Wimbledon postcode? (This is going to be really easy if you live there, obviously, unless of course you're really stupid.)

3 Fred Perry is famous now for fitting out mods with designer fighting wear. He also invented the sweatband, dated Marlene Dietrich and won Wimbledon. How many times did he do this? (Win Wimbledon, I mean not invent the sweatband, you can only invent the sweatband once, or date Marlene Dietrich.)

4 Tennis-elbow-suffering pop pensioner Cliff Richard made the rain much worse one year by getting up and singing an impromptu set in front of the punters waiting for the rain and the old bastard to stop. What year was this? And what was the date?

5 Unbelievably, there are tennis tournaments other than Wimbledon – though none of them really count – you know there's even one in Australia? Do you know in which month this is held?

Answers

1 See your answer.

2 SW19. Even the postcode sounds posh.

3 He won it three times. Did you hear that Tim? Three times. Greg? Andy? Three times!

4 3 July 1996, which is now also known as 'Black Wednesday'. For some reason the BBC feel compelled to repeat this whenever it rains even though it happened long enough ago to be forgotten.

5 January. Get off, you can't play tennis in January, the grass will be too wet, surely? Aussies, eh.

41 Numbers

....

Wake up your nerd, we've got more numbers for you now!

1 Fractions are a bastard. Next to no one can add them, and now there's calculators there's little point. But you're not getting off doing fractions: what's 3/4 + 4/5 - 3/7? Put your mobile phones away NOW!!

2 Women's tennis eh? Oof. Blimey. I don't know where to look. And then there's the grunting and squealing. Oof. The thing is, they play a game of tennis too. Oof. What's the number of points you need to win a straight-sets love match in the women's singles at Wimbledon?

3 How many top-notch pop rockers do you get from the following sum (classic line-ups only): the Beatles + Queen + the Who + Led Zeppelin - Coldplay = ?

4 Time ticks on, ever on, and we drag slowly towards the grave. Sorry, got a bit dark there for a moment. How many minutes are there in a week?

5 Addition: add up all the answers in this round and what do you get?

Answers

1 1 17/140. Bravo if you got that.

2 48 points. Four points a game, twelve games. That's forty-eight grunts and squeaks.

3 Twelve.

4 10080.

5 10141 17/140. If you got that, give yourself a biscuit.

42 Art: actually, paintings, alright??

Art eh? I know nothing about art, and the more I learn, the less I like. It's a long time since painters were expected to paint pictures of actual things, rather than just crap in a bucket and call it *The Decline of Western Civilisation II: Steve's House*. Is this because they've decided that painting has had its day or because they can't paint? You decide, but hurry up, what's in the bucket is beginning to hum.

1   This classic painting by William Frederick Yeames depicts a heart-rending scene from the Civil War. He painted it in 1878 – what is it called? Full title only please.

2 This classic painting is by who, of what, and more importantly, who won?

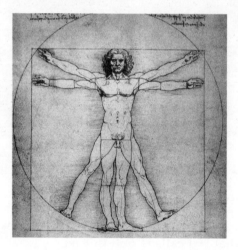

3 Leonardo da Vinci painted the *Mona Lisa,* which for some reason is the most famous painting in the world. I have no idea why, and I'm sure no one else does, it's just one of those things isn't it? Like the way you're meant to like the Beach Boys as much as the Beatles when really they're a bit shit (and that high singing is embarrassing). But he also did another famous picture – here it is. It's called *Vitruvian Man* and what is it meant to represent?

4 This painting is known as *The Laughing Cavalier* but who is it by?

5 Roy Lichtenstein is most famous for his Pop Art style, which saw him taking comic book images and blowing them up much larger than the originals. We've all seen that one called Whaaaaam! With the fighter plane blowing something up. Whoo-pi-bloody do, nice one mate, give yourself a biscuit, you copied something out of a comic. Lichtenstein also ... Actually you know what? Sod it, what's my favourite colour?

Answers

1 It's called: *And When Did You Last See Your Father?*

I need the full title or I cannot accept the answer! If you missed off the '*And*' I'm afraid you don't get your points. The poor lad, his dad's gone and the nasty Roundheads want to know where he is. I haven't seen my boy for nine years now, so thanks for bringing that up.

2 It's JMW Turner's *The Battle of Trafalgar*. And we won, twenty-seven British ships took on thirty-three French and Spanish ships, destroying twenty-two enemy ships for the loss of no British ones. Stitch that Boney!!!

3 It's meant to represent perfect human proportions. And that's bonkers. Have another look. That's way too big.

4 It's by Frans Hals, he was Dutch. What I like about it is this painting is of a bloke, nothing ambiguous about it. With a cheeky smile. I reckon he looks like a great fella to have a pint with, you know, someone you could chew the cud with, set the world to rights whilst supping on life's finest ales. All this from a painting. I'm so alone.

5 Maroon, the colour of service.

43 Shane Richie

With a showbiz career that spans more than two decades, Shane 'The Legend' Richie is an actor, singer, television presenter and media personality. His career in many ways is the one Darren Day wishes he had had (instead he sleeps in his car from time to time). Sorry Daz. But what do you know of 'The Legend'?*

1 Shane Richie joined flagship BBC1 soap opera *EastEnders* in 2002, bringing his unique style and charisma to the show, gripping audiences with plotlines around his character's turbulent love life with Kat Slater (played by Jessie Wallace). What was the name of Shane's character, who was specially written for him?

2 In 2009 Shane starred as Archie Daley in Channel 5's relaunch of which flagship British TV drama classic?

3 In 2008 Shane hosted Sky One's flagship music-lyrics quiz show. What was it called?

4 In 1994 Shane hosted ITV's flagship morning Pictionary-based celebrity quiz show. What was it called?

5 Shane Richie will be returning to flagship BBC1 soap opera EastEnders to play whom?

---

* OK mate, here's the mention you were promised in full. You owe me a pint, minimum.

Answers

1 Alfie Moon. They wrote the part for him specially.

2 *Minder*. We await a second series.

3 *Don't Forget The Lyrics*. It did what it said on the tin. We await the second series.

4 *Win, Lose or Draw*. He took over from Danny Baker, you know.

5 Alfie Moon. Pay attention. They wrote the part for him specially.

44 The Human Bean Body

The human bean body is an amazing machine, capable of thousands of actions all at once, and is able to repair itself. It's a truly wondrous natural structure, which is why we are able to go out every weekend and push it to its limit, filling it with booze and kebabs, safe in the knowledge that it can cope. Until we die.

1 The intestine is the canal that connects your stomach to your anus, or if that's too medical, your guts to your bumhole. In fact I'll stop calling it intestines and refer to it as the poo-pipe. The poo-pipe is split into two different bits: the large poo-pipe and the small poo-pipe. It's the latter I'm concerned with. I would like to know how long (in feet of course, back off Brussels) the small poo-pipe is?

2 Rapid eye movement, or REM, is a physiological occurrence that takes place during the part of the sleep cycle when people dream. It's common to refer to this stage of sleep as REM sleep. What is the name of the guitarist in REM?

3 Expel wind, blow off, fart, trump, tread on a duck, the leather cheerio bark, low-flying geese, cut the cheese, guff, grunt, whatever you want to call it, we all do it. Even Abbey Clancy. What I want to know is how many times a year on average does the human bean fart? I'll accept a hundred either way of the answer I have here.

4 My heart has been broken so many times, on so many occasions, I'm surprised it can still pump blood around my loveless body, and it's only thanks to booze that it doesn't hurt any more. I just want to feel something. The heart is divided into four chambers. Name all four of them for a point.

5 The human brain is the command centre for the entire central nervous system and is over three times the size of the typical mammal brain. It is very different to the typical mammal brain in the sense that the different sexes use it in different ways. Men think with the right side of the brain, but which side of the brain do woman think with?

(Answers on page 104)

Time for another pint . . .

Watch Out for the Know-All

We know this bloke. He stands at the quiz machine hitting the buttons in a blur. You've hardly read the question yourself and he's already got the answer. He's burning his way through the machine, so he's a dead cert for when you chuck together your team. But proceed cautiously. Because he will have an Achilles heel. For while he may be hot on Greek mythology, or history, or geography, or politics, he knows nothing about *Coronation Street*. When it comes to football, his mind is a blank. Don't even try to get him to answer about *EastEnders*. Because what will always happen, without fail, is that once he's on your team you'll run into the *Corrie/EastEnders*/Premiership round of death, without a mention of Agamemnon in sight, and your team will sink without a trace. Remember that above all, it's a team, and there's no 'geek' in 'team'.

Answers

1 22 feet. Which is about 7m squared – Oi! No metric!

2 Peter Buck.

3 5110. Christ, imagine them all at once. It would have your trousers off. Mind you, the average takes into account women who never do, or so they claim, so maybe it's blokes doing all the wind-work.

4 Left atria and right atria, right ventricle and left ventricle. Although I think mine has more pieces than crazy paving.

5 The wrong side. What? Don't give her a map is all I'm saying.

45 Colours

Here's more questions of colour. That came out wrong.

1 Listen up nerds! Here's one for you! Which colour is evoked by light having a spectrum dominated by energy with a wavelength of roughly 440–490 nanometres?

2 Belgium, Jeremy Clarkson's favourite country (well it must be, he mentions it every five minutes on *Top Gear* doesn't he? He's obsessed) has a flag, believe it or not, though I doubt they salute to the thing or anything, you wouldn't would you? Describe the Belgian flag.

3 Which colour was a top two hit in 1981? Top two means it got to number two. Not that it got to number one. You wouldn't call it top two if it had got to number one, would you?

4 'Richard Of York Gave Battle In Vain' is how some people remember the visual spectrum of colour: Red Orange Yellow Green Blue Indigo Violet. Richard Of York Gave Battle In Vain. Clever eh? Of course you could just remember the colours. Where did Richard Of York Give Battle In Vain?

5 Which came first, the orange fruit or the colour orange? That's a question worth asking, but not one you'd ever ask in a pub quiz because no one knows for sure. In British history, who was William III of Orange married to?

Answers

1 It's blue. The colour associated with sadness, which is why nerds know the answer.

2 It's a tricolour of black, gold and red horizontal stripes. In that order. Not entirely unlike the German flag. I'm just saying.

3 'Golden Brown'.

4 The Battle of Bosworth Field. Which doesn't help you remember anything.

5 Queen Mary II. He traded up.

46 Superheroes and Other Nonsense

We don't have superheroes in this country, mainly because we have a history of our own, unlike the Americans, who invented superheroes because the only people in their past are George Washington and a load of cowboys who were either bank robbers or genocidal. My name's Ben Elton, thank you and goodnight*.

1 Peter Parker, the Amazing Spiderman, got his powers how?

2 Name the Fantastic Four. There's four of them, so it's a question that is arguably easier than the seven dwarves, and only marginally less childish.

3 Superman flies around in his underpants, can see through women's clothing, can burn stuff with his eyes and freeze stuff with his breath. He's also very strong. He fights for Truth, Justice and The American Way, almost as if they're different things. What is his Kryptonian name?

4 The Incredibles are stars of the movie of the same name, *The Incredibles*, in which they work as a superhero team called the Incredibles. What is Mr Incredible's name?

5 Complete the following song lyric: ner ner ner ner, ner ner ner ner, ner ner ner ner, ner ner ner ner ...

---

* He wrote the Queen musical *We Will Rock You*, so for all that lefty stuff the boy came good in the end.

Answers

1 By being bitten by a radioactive spider. Like I said, nonsense.

2 Reed Richards aka Mr Fantastic, Susan 'Storm' Richards aka The Invisible Woman, Johnny Storm aka The Human Torch, Ben Grimm aka The Thing. Grow up. One point if you got all four, it's childish.

3 Kal-El.

4 Bob Parr. Not Mr Incredible. Sorry.

5 Batman

47 Reality TV Firsts

Reality TV is no such thing. Take that jungle programme. I mean, how real is the scenario in which a Learjet full of G-listers crashes in the Australian bush and is then picked off one by one by two Geordie hobbits? And *Hell's Kitchen*: seeing as celebrities don't do a stroke of work and are bunch of soft-handed timewasters, why would anyone imagine that they could string a meal together in a proper kitchen? What a load of bollocks. But bollocks that rules the world.

1 *Big Brother*, remember that? The show that relentlessly puked up a succession of wankers, idiots, morons and desperados* and for which there seemed to be an unending supply of willing victims. Thank God it's not on any more. Who won the first series of *Big Brother*?

2 *I'm A Celebrity … Get Me Out Of Here!* is a show in which people who aren't celebrities don't get out of anywhere, seeing as there's a hotel up the road. But if we're honest it's the best of the formats, as at least something happens. It's a life-changing event; it can make or break a career and propel you to new heights. Who won the first series of this show?

3 *Castaway* was the BBC's reality show, though they didn't call it that because they're posh, they called it a social experiment. They bunged a load of earnest people on an island to see what would happen. Ant and Dec were nowhere to be seen. They lived in turf-covered eco pods for Chrissakes. Who won it?

4 *Hell's Kitchen* is a classic of the reality format. The idea that Barry McGuigan might cook you a lemon soufflé is irresistible if you're the sort of person who makes TV,

---

* I wish I could say they were berks, but berks are, well, likeable.

but when you're sat there eating it and it's taken three hours to arrive and it's salty, you might end up wanting to kill someone. Who won the first series of *Hell's Kitchen*?

5 *The Apprentice* is the BBC's premier reality show from America, fronted by Alan Sugar sitting in for Donald Trump. Altogether now: Nu nu nu nu nu nu nu nu nu nu nu nu nu nuuuuuur! What a bunch of knuckleheads, chumps and donuts they get on that show. If they're such genius business people why aren't they millionaires? That's not the question. Who won the first series of *The Apprentice*?

(Answers on page 112)

The Halfway Mark

It's halfway through the evening. The quizmaster has decided it's time to take a break. You hand in your score sheets. This part of the evening is a raw combination of relief and tension; relief that you've made it this far without dropping any proper clangers, and tension because you have no idea how the other teams have fared. That lot over the other side of the pub with the old bloke, they seem to exude confidence, and the week before last they stole that chicken, stole it from under your noses because your knowledge of golf let you down. The problem with golf is all anyone knows is bad jokes about Tiger Woods and, not only that, they're *old* bad jokes about Tiger Woods. This is the moment to get a couple more in, to go to the bog, to make final decisions on the questions that are still up in the air. Waste this time, and you could regret it for the rest of your life. Well, the rest of the evening, maybe. But I'm trying to make a point here.

An honourable team would not listen to what the other teams are muttering and whispering, an honourable team would not in fact have a designated eavesdropper whose sole role on the team was listening to what the other teams might be saying, but as pub quiz crimes go it hardly ranks alongside using your mobile phone. When you get to the toilet, you have to weigh carefully the kind of contact you make with those around you – for all you know, the way you stand at the urinal or what you hum to yourself whilst engaged in your business may well subconsciously alert the opponent to an answer. You might find the sit-downs to all be mysteriously locked as cheats (who seldom prosper!) text for answers in a desperate last-minute bid to stall handing in their sheet. But as you prepare for part two of the quiz, take a look around you – how do the other teams look? Has anyone actually left? (this rarely happens, but when it does the disgraced team know they are taking the longest walk of all and can never return to that gaff because the solid stench of failure will forever hang over them like a cloud of Icelandic volcanic ash). And then come the scores – the moment of truth, the standings before you enter part two, aka the home straight. How much work have you still got to do? What did you get wrong? What did you get right? Who's to blame? Who's been getting it right all this time. Some teams tear themselves to pieces with blame and recrimination, even at this middle stage, spitting bitter words of hatred over wrongly answered movie questions. But good luck because we're going in again anyway ... See you at the final scores.

Answers

1 Craig. That Scouse bloke. He had a DIY show for a bit. Then vanished. Bless him.

2 Tony Blackburn. Remember him? He went back to doing radio.

3 Celebrity Labrador Ben Fogle. You know if you throw a ball he goes and gets it. They brought *Castaway* back in 2007 and no one watched it.

4 Scouse songbird, actor, dancer and erstwhile swimsuit modellist Jennifer Ellison.

5 Timothy Campbell. No, me either.

48 Who Are You?

Below is a selection of questions on one-hit wonders, knuckleheads and chancers that you may or may not have forgotten about.

1 Thankfully Channel 4 has canned *Big Brother*, that awful show that people go on in a desperate attempt to become famous, and then when they've finished the show moan about how all the other contestants are going on the show just to become famous. Which never-heard-of-since chancer won the second series of UK *Big Brother*?

2 The Germans are not known for their successful pop music, but more for starting wars*. A German did have a hit in this country in 1984 with a song called '99 Red Balloons', – a song all about a war getting started. Give it a rest! They're obsessed. But who was it?

3 Why people want to be politicians is far beyond me, you get to achieve nothing but being really unpopular. Some people go into it thinking they are going to change the world and others go into it just to waste everybody's time. David Sutch or Screaming Lord Sutch as he called himself started his own political party, but what was it called?

4 Britpop was on the whole a huge disappointment and, apart from a couple of groups, produced a shedload of rubbish. One God-awful band in 1995 released an irritating, whiny song called 'Daydreamer', which didn't have much of a melody and just involved a load of pouting by grown men. Who released this song?

5 *EastEnders* is the greatest sitcom on television and has been for decades now. Twice a week I howl with laughter at its depiction of everyday London folk. Pauline

---

* They started it. They did.

Fowler's daughter Michelle was married and had a baby with a character called Lofty. Which actor played Lofty?

Answers

1 Brian Dowling. Remember him? No me neither and if you do remember him, maybe you need to have a word with yourself.

2 Nena. Remember her? No me neither.

3 Official Monster Raving Loony Party. Remember them? No me neither.

4 Menswear. Remember them? No me neither.

5 Tom Watt. Remember him? No me neither.

49 Disney Films

More Disney films. You've seen 'em all, you've been brainwashed into submission by them, you've fallen asleep in front of them countless times, but how much have you actually taken in?

1   A tough one for you now. For all their films, only one Disney movie has been nominated for Best Picture at the Oscars, because their films are for children. Stands to reason. Which is the only Disney film to have been nominated for an Oscar for Best Picture?

2   *Pocahontas* is the heartwarming tale of cartoon Red Indians versus cartoon Brits and a cartoon romance that springs up between the main two cartoon characters, Pocahontas and Captain John Smith. I used to nod off before Captain Smith began to learn that the Indians are not savages like in *Avatar*. I miss my boy that's all. Who voiced Captain Smith?

3   *The Lion King* is the one Elton John wrote the music for. 'Circle of Life', all that blah blah, 'Hakuna Matata' etc etc. Who wrote the words?

4   *Alice in Wonderland* is a classic Disney film that doesn't follow the book all that faithfully, if we're honest, but who cares? Disney didn't and it did very nicely for him at the box office, so there. And it's all psychedelical and that. What year was it released?

5   I knew I said I wouldn't ask this but, sod it, name the seven dwarves. Get on with it. Easy.

Answers

1 *Beauty and the Beast.* Didn't win it though. *Silence of the Lambs* won it, which is not a kids' film.

2 Mel Gibson, before he stuck his oar in with *Braveheart*.

3 Sir Tim Rice. Never was a knighthood better bestowed. Top bloke.

4 1951. I've not seen the new one with Johnny Depp in it. Irish Geoff's DVD supplier hasn't cracked 3D yet.

5 Doc, Grumpy, Happy, Sleepy, Bashful, Sneezy and Dopey. There are all sorts of rumours.

50 Prime Ministers

More power-hungry politicos. The people responsible for how we've ended up in the shit over and over again. Who we voted for. Hmmmm.

1 William Pitt the Younger was so called because he was young when he became Prime Minister (though it wasn't called that at the time, that's what it was, before a fight breaks out). How young was he?

2 The Duke of Wellington: top bloke, he defeated Napoleon. Not only that, he was Prime Minister for two years. On his watch the Catholic Emancipation Bill happened. What did the Duke do over this Bill?

3 The Liberals eh? Not a lot you can say about them without causing a pub fight. That's why we don't do politics in my gaff. Ever. But who was the last Liberal Prime Minister?

4 Which Prime Minister brought in the Cones Hotline, 08457 504030?

5 Robert Peel (no, no relation to John) is famous for, amongst other things, beginning the police (who in their right mind would give Sting work?) This frankly doesn't deserve celebrating but has been, in a number of statues. How many of them are there in the UK?

Answers

1 24. Imagine that! 24. A graduate trainee, in charge!
What did he know? Nothing! He'd never poured a pint
in his life.

2 He fought a duel. Yeah, stitch that Gordon Brown!

3 David Lloyd George, the Welsh Wizard. The last Liberal
coincided with everyone getting the vote. Coincidence?
Ha! Although we now have a Liberal Deputy Prime
Minister. Who'd have thought it eh? None of the
newspapers or pundits who got the whole thing totally
wrong.

4 John Major. Donut.

5 Eleven. Eleven! That's nearly as many as Churchill isn't
it? Still, he had a tank named after him and you can't
defend a country with a statue, just ask Saddam.

51 Numbers

More numbers for you now. Come on, you know you love it.

1 VAT is a bastard. Why can't a plumber just tell you what he is actually going to cost rather than then cheekily adding 'plus VAT'? What was the rate of VAT by the time Gordon Brown was done with wrecking the economy?

2 The Devil knows it. Loonies and the Pope know it. Iron Maiden know it. Kids at metal concerts know it. Do you know it? What is the number of the Beast?

3 What is the number of the Beast, plus VAT? The VAT you're charging being what you thought it was in question 1.

4 The Queen Mother, when she was with us, seemed as though she was going to go on for ever. But she didn't. How old was she when she passed on, shuffled off, departed?

5 Dalmations + Trumpton Firemen - Dwarfs + how old Lady Di was when her candle in the wind went out =?

Answers

1 Who cares? It doesn't matter, pay cash. But it was 17.5%.

2 666. Everyone knows that.

3 782.55. There must be VAT in Hell, if only to keep the accountants busy. Mind you, they like it.

4 101. Dalmations. That would be the clue. But I don't do clues.

5 101 + 6 - 7 + 36 = 136. Pugh, Pugh, Barney McGrew, Cuthbert, Dibble, Grubb.

52 Glam Rock!

The music time should have forgot. In fact the music
time should never have thought about in the first place

Glam rock, when you look back at it, makes no sense at all, unless
you use it as a way of explaining what happened to all the drugs
left over from the sixties. Why would fourteen-year-old girls scream
at a man in platform shoes, glittery trousers and huge mutton chops?
Apart from out of fear, horror and bewilderment? But at one point
glam rock ruled the world. Mind you it was a very different world.
It's no coincidence that now there's other things to do, no one buys
glam rock records any more.

1 The Bay City Rollers dressed in ludicrous tartan (as if
there's any other kind; there's always some nerk at a
wedding pretending to be Scottish), played glam rock/
pop and, for some reason that still remains a mystery,
dominated the charts for a couple of years. They even
had a TV show. What was it called?

2 Gary Glitter. Well tricky this one. How do you ask a
question about him without causing a kerfuffle? By
asking a question about the KLF. Which KLF number
one hit sampled Gary Glitter?

3 David Bowie saw glam rock coming and joined in with
the whole thing, becoming Ziggy Stardust, even though
he must in his heart have known that his greatest work
–'Under Pressure' – with Queen was still a few years off.
Which of his hits shared a riff with 'Blockbuster'? Not
Blockbusters with Bob Holness, 'Blockbuster' by the
Sweet.

4 Everyone loves Wizzard's somewhat ill-thought-out
Christmas hit 'I Wish It Could Be Christmas Every Day',
even though, if you think it through, Christmas every day
would be more ruinous economically than another five
years of Gordon Brown. Everyone buying presents but no
one going to work – unsustainable. When was it a hit?

5 ELO – remember them? 'Mister Blue Sky'? Can't think of any others, sorry. What does ELO stand for?

Answers

1 *Shang-a-Lang.* Apparently they did comedy sketches etc. Gawd.

2 'Doctorin' The Tardis'. Doctor Who-oo, The Tardis! Doctor Who-oo, The Tardis! They don't write them like that any more, mainly because the KLF retired.

3 'The Jean Genie'.

4 1973.

5 Electric Light Orchestra.

53 Currency

Pounds sterling is the finest legal tender in the world, no questions asked. Other currencies just don't cut the mustard as far as buying things in Britain is concerned and are therefore pretty useless. 'In for a penny, in for a dollar'? I think not. 'A euro of flesh?' Back off Brussels. If you look at the dictionary definition of sterling, you will find phrases like 'of the highest quality', 'genuine and reliable', and 'first-class', which says it all really.

1 Sterling *is* the finest currency, but in which year did it take one step nearer to becoming the euro by getting all decimalised?

2 In their last known act of cowardice, France ditched their currency the franc and replaced it with the Euro. On which day in which year did they begin using the euro?

3 Benjamin Franklin is known to the Americans as one of the 'Founding Fathers of the United States'. To everyone else he is known as 'that bloke who invented the flexible urinary catheter'. He'd definitely thought about it. On which dollar bill (that's a note, by the way) is his face found?

4 The Aussies took their eye off the ball in 1966 and changed their Australian pound sterling to the Australian dollar. An insensible move of some lunacy, you'll agree. And since then they've all been coming over here to re-live the glory days of the pound. Despite that, they still have a beautiful British woman on their $5 note. Who is it?

5 You've got to feel sorry for the Cambodians, they've not had a great time in recent history, have they? Let's be honest, that's what happens when you let the French run the place. What is the name of the currency used in Cambodia?

Answers

1 1971, a dark year for Britain (the birth of Jessie Wallace, to name just one other catastrophe in that year).

2 1 January 1999.

3 $100. Since the US caused that massive global recession, this note hasn't been circulating that much.

4 Queen Elizabeth II. And on the other side is a picture of an Aussie building that drags its value down. They're their own worst enemy.

5 The Cambodian riel. I will also accept the US dollar, blackmail and being nudged in the ribs with an AK-47.

54 Who's Who?

By now you should have got the idea that this Who's Who round is nothing to do with Doctor Who. In fact, it wearies me to have to mention it again. It's questions asking you who people are.

1 *1984* was George Orwell's nightmare vision of the future. But when it came to nightmares he had no idea what he was talking about, because nowhere in his book does he mention the horrendous, soul-searing sound of Duran Duran. Maybe this was because he had confused himself by using a pen name. What was George Orwell's real name?

2 Allen Stewart Konigsberg is who? Who is Allen Stewart Konigsberg?

3 'I'm the dandy highwayman so sick of easy fashion' etc blah blah sang self-regarding bonkers pop fop Adam Ant. But guess what – that's not his real name. What's Adam Ant's real name?

4 Who in God's name is James Newell Osterberg, Jr.? If you get this one I'll buy you a pint. Jesus.

5 Who is Jordan? Consider your answer carefully.

Answers

1 Eric Arthur Blair.

2 Woody Allen. I'd change it too. German name – no one would expect you to be funny, would they?

3 Stuart Leslie Goddard.

4 It's Iggy Pop.

5 Deduct all points you scored in this round if you know who she is.

55 Formula 1

Your Sunday lunch has just gone down, so what better way to aid digestion than by waving your fist at the TV and shouting 'Get over!' at a bunch of overpaid tax-dodging playboys? F1 – it's the greatest sport in the world.

1 How many women – to date – have driven in Formula 1? And get this – the answer's not none.

2 Which team fielded a six-wheeled car in 1976? Let's be honest, it's the kind of thing you might make with your Lego.

3 James Hunt was a top-flight British driver, playboy, posh bloke and totty magnet who didn't care, a general all-round eccentric of the racetrack. What was his racing nickname? Though being posh he probably called it a soubriquet*.

4 Which racing driver was known as Mr Monaco on account of his being really, really good at the Monaco track, obviously?

5 Ayrton Senna – who gave his name for all eternity to rhyming slang for the ten-pound note – was driving for Williams when he met his untimely in Italy in 1994. Who was the other driver who died the day before in testing?

---

* French word.

Answers

1 Five. Sadly they all scraped the car parking it on a bollard none of them saw etc etc.

2 Tyrrell. Remember them? No. They got a one-two at the Swedish Grand Prix. Later on, the rules were changed saying you were only allowed four wheels, probably because six is silly.

3 Hunt the Shunt. See what they did there? Brilliant ha ha ha.

4 Graham Hill. Damon's dad. He won it five times in the 1960s when the crash barriers were straw bales that would catch fire if you so much as sneezed at them. Nails. He had a neat little 'tache as well not unlike Dick Dastardly.

5 Roland Ratzenberger. All smart remarks about Rat-fans should be put aside please.

• •

**The 80s was an appalling time: the music, hair and fashion were
all embarrassing and no amount of forced nostalgia about that
decade will make me feel otherwise or make me want to watch _Dirty
Dancing_. God I hate those talking-heads shows with Shane Richie***
going on about how good the 80s were.

1 The only thing anyone ever remembers about Live Aid
was Queen. None of the rest of them needed to bother
turning up. In which year did Freddie and the boys rock
Wembley Stadium at this event?

2 Princess Diana was a candle in the wind and was
definitely killed by a French bloke. She had two sons,
Girl-face and the ginger one. Which one was born 15
September 1984?

3 Bucks Fizz were Britain's poor – no, stony broke – man's
answer to ABBA, who weren't that good themselves, so
you can imagine just how bad Bucks Fizz were. People
only really remember them for the skirt-ripping-off
thing. For one point, name all four original members of
Bucks Fizz.

4 I reckon I could run a marathon if I wanted to, but I
don't so I haven't tried. But I could if I wanted to and
I reckon on my day I could outrun Daley Thompson.
Anyway, in which year was the first London marathon?

5 Argentina started the Falklands war that we had to
finish, by invading British soil. Bang out of order lads.
What was the date of this invasion?

---

* Another mention for you there, mate.

Answers

1 1985. Live Aid-ruining band Duran Duran played at the US concert and totally ruined it. You've never witnessed true pain until you've seen Simon Le Bon slalom round the right notes during 'A View To A Kill' at Live Aid. That bloke couldn't carry a tune even if it was gaffer-taped to his hand.

2 The ginger one. I like him though, top bloke. He has the best job in the world, he gets to hang out and do whatever he wants and all he has to do is stand on a balcony and not throw up.

3 Bobby G, Cheryl Baker, Mike Nolan and Jay Aston.

4 1981. Timewasters. Sundays are for sitting in beer gardens.

5 Friday, 2 April 1982. Never forgive, never forget. And a Friday, another weekend totalled.

57 Pot Luck

Get used to it, it's a selection of random questions.

1   Keith Moon, Moon the Loon, Moonie, etc, played the drums for the Who until he received his call-up papers for God's great band in the sky (they'd managed for quite a while without a drummer and then Moonie and Bonzo turn up within two years of each other, nightmare). Which brand of beautiful British drums did he play?

2   Walkers crisps are the best crisps of the lot, without a doubt, especially ready salted. Worcester sauce are wrong. Totally wrong. Maybe a drop of it in your spag bol, but not a whole packet of crisps. What colour are Walkers ready salted crisp packets?

3   Gary Lineker is without a doubt one of the greatest footballers of all time. And he's great on the telly too, especially now he doesn't have to do *They Think It's All Over* and sit there with that pained expression. He won the Golden Shoe in the World Cup too. Which year?

4   King Henry III wasn't the best of kings, but the poor sod came to the throne when he was nine and was pretty clueless. Fair enough. Don't blame the boy, he was about the same age as my kid, who I haven't seen now for nine years, thanks for bringing that up. Rebels queued up to have a pop, and we even ended up with a parliament as a result. Thanks for that. Who was the main rebel who set up parliament?

5   What links the last four questions? Keith Moon's drums, Walkers ready salted, Lineker, the creator of parliament?

Answers

1 Premier, from Leicester.

2 Red. And Walkers are from Leicester.

3 1986. He scored six goals. And he's from Leicester.

4 Simon De Montfort. Earl of Leicester.

5 It's Leicester, as the bloke reading the answers knows. And there you are, four interesting things about Leicester. This book is value for money, you can't argue with that.

∙ ∙

The 70s were an era of self indulgence, flares, prog rock, punk rock, power cuts, strikes, and all that other stuff people who were around then crap on about. It is also the decade that brought us Queen though, so it can't have all been bad.

1 Which hit BBC no-nonsense cop TV series, based around the nonsense of time travel, is set in the 1970s?

2 Which war ended in 1973 with the Paris Peace Accords? I suppose if you're going to do peace accords anywhere Paris would be the place, though the French will be advising you to surrender.

3 Concorde eh? A superb combination of British engines, and French, well no one knows which bit they made and I won't be saying know how. They don't fly Concorde any more even though it meant Joan Collins could leave the country more quickly and a good thing too. When did the first Concorde commercial flights start?

4 The Pope, eh? Who'd want that job? All that power and you still have wear a frock. No thanks. And nowadays having to deal with all those kiddie fiddlers. Anyway, who did Pope John Paul I succeed in 1978?

5 The 70s was a top-notch time for nerds. You had *Star Trek* movies, you had *Star Wars* films starting (and don't tell me for one minute he planned the sequels – how come Darth Vader in the first film acts like he's never heard of Luke Skywalker if he's his dad? Total cobblers), but you also had space travel actually happening. Which probe revealed Jupiter's rings (stop sniggering at the back) in 1979?

Answers

1   *Life on Mars.* Top bloke that Gene Hunt, though he's a bit leftwing for my taste.

2   The Vietnam War. The Americans didn't lose the Vietnam War, never forget that. They agreed to leave Vietnam, remove all their soldiers and not come back, but only because they were all needed on film sets to make Vietnam War movies.

3   21 January 1976. I'll take 1976, which is a one-in-ten chance if we're honest.

4   Pope Paul VI. Then JP I dropped dead and JP II took over, then they got the German.

5   Voyager I. It's still out there, probably with a dodgy picture of a hairy 70s bloke like out of *The Joy of Sex* on it in case the aliens find it. No wonder they haven't made contact.

59 TV Chefs

More TV chefs. There's nothing I like more than sitting down in front of the TV with beans on toast watching someone else slave away in the kitchen making food I'd never dream of eating on the grounds that it's not normal.

1   James Martin is that Yorkshire pudding of a bloke on Saturday mornings who's far too bright and breezy first thing for anyone who had a proper Friday night. What do they cook as quick as they can at the end of the show in speedy *Top Gear* style?

2   Gordon Ramsay did a trial for a football club or something, no one quite remembers, but there we go. The papers printed it loads of times without checking it, oh dear what a pity never mind. He's also well known for swearing. What is the punningly hilarious name of his show on Channel 4?

3   Sundays are a strange day for TV. You're basically hanging on for the game in the afternoon, or the F1 GP, and then before lunch that bloke Lovejoy crops up in a skinny jumper, and falls off an electric skateboard or something (it's that or the *Hollyoaks* omnibus, but my TV doesn't switch to Channel 4 on principle). What is the name of the pickled-onion-headed chef on *Something For the Weekend*?

4   Antony Worrall Thompson is the short one who sort of grumbles his way through stuff as if he can't quite be bothered. Who described him as 'a squashed Bee Gee'?

5   Marco Pierre White: half French, half Italian, half English. How is that possible? (That's not the question). He advertises stock cubes. For whom?

Answers

1 An omelette.

2 It's *The F Word*, see? Food. See? I love it!!!

3 Simon Rimmer. Another punning name. Ha ha, I love it!

4 Gordon Ramsay. Which for him is pretty restrained. I'm surprised he didn't call him a '******* ****'. Or a '*****'. Or 'a total ****'. Or a 'complete and utter total ******* ****'. Sorry, I'm still laughing at *The F Word*.

5 Knorr.

60 Sayings

People love a good saying. They're always saying them, especially old people and plumbers. Half the time no one knows what they mean, but they say them anyway. Sayings, phrases, idioms, clichés or expressions, whatever you call them, this round deals with them. Complete these well-known and horribly overused sentences.

1 Here's the first one. Don't know if you know, but complete the following: 'Hunger is a good ...'

2 We all know this one: 'Absence makes the heart ...'

3 These are getting easier. Though if you say 'Ooh I know this,' and then get it wrong – well, you'll see. 'Pride comes ...'

4 How are you getting on? You must know this one, even though the answer's wrong, you have to get it right. ' The way to a man's heart is ...'

5 And finally, 'All is fair in ...

Answers

1 'Hunger is a good sauce.' No it's not, ketchup is a good sauce, with chips, but never with roast. English mustard goes well with beef and lamb and brown sauce with fry-ups. But hunger isn't a sauce, it's not. Salad cream is a sauce, as is mayonnaise at a push, but not once have I been in the supermarket and found a jar of hunger in the condiment aisle. Never, not once.

2 'Absence makes the heart grow fonder.' This simply isn't true. I haven't seen my wife since she left me and took my boy and I hate her more and more with every single day that passes. Half of everything!?!? Lawyers and their bloody compromises! Thanks for bringing that up.

3 'Pride comes before a fall.' Again, this is nonsense, the thing that comes before a fall is normally a trip or a fight.

4 'The way to a man's heart is through his stomach.' No, it's through his chest. What sort of thing is that to teach to trainee doctors? No wonder the NHS is on its bloody knees. Women say they understand men, but when they say stuff like 'A man's brain is between his legs', they clearly don't. Mind you that might answer why the women I meet never look down there.

5 'All is fair in love and war.' Again this isn't true, you try telling that to Poland.

61 The Theatre

God help us, the theatre. No one likes it, no one. They say they do, but they don't. And try putting on a play that says Maggie Thatcher was a good thing and everyone'll call you rude names and flounce out. But we the British have the greatest theatre in the world, so here's some questions about it. Though I might be sick.

1   William Shakespeare was the greatest playwright the world has ever seen, even though no one can understand a word of any of his plays. Especially not the people in them, who say the stuff without a clue about what's going on. Which play contains this quote: 'All the world's a stage, and all the men and women merely players: they have their exits and their entrances; and one man in his time plays many parts . . . '? Meaningless.

2   Harold Pinter was, until he died, Britain's greatest living playwright. His plays were full of pauses, that's pretty much all I know about him. What was the name of the play that made him a star on the London theatrical scene in 1957?

3   Susan Boyle eh? Whatever happened to her? No one knows. She sang a song on *Britain's Got Talent* called 'I Dreamed a Dream', the kind of title that is made of pure so-what. That's like saying 'I Walked A Walk', or 'I Bummed a Bum' (maybe not the second one). Which theatre show was that song from?

4   Which long-running play contains the following characters: Maureen Lyon, Mollie Ralston, Giles Ralston, Christopher Wren, Mrs Boyle, Major Metcalf, Miss Casewell, Mr Paravicini and Detective Sergeant Trotter?

5   Andrew Lloyd Webber. That's not a question, but he's certainly had the British public scratching their heads for a long time now. His really big improbable hit was *Jesus Christ Superstar*. Who wrote the words?

Answers

1 *As You Like It* which, as it happens, I don't. No one does.

2 *The Birthday Party.* Yeah, me neither.

3 *Les Miserables,* an everyday story of miserable French people. As if there's any other kind. It's been running for twenty-five years or something. Make it stop.

4 It's *The Mousetrap.* I won't tell you who did the murder but it's an amazing earth-shattering twist that no one would ever guess that it's the copper. They tell you not to tell anyone, but it's been running since 1952 so it was bound to get out.

5 It was Sir Tim Rice. He's a top bloke and deserves a mention. He did *The Lion King* too. Top bloke. Won't hear a word against him. Wears that knighthood lightly.

62 The 70s Again   1970s

· ·

Here they are, more questions about the 70s. Just be grateful
these questions aren't going on for a whole decade like the 70s
themselves.

1 The 70s were chock full of coups and kidnappings and
   stuff, all kinds of stuff going on. Not here though in
   Great Britain because everyone was on strike or busy
   making rubbish motors, and couldn't be bothered with
   any of that. Which country had a Carnation Revolution
   that restored democracy in April 1974?

2 In lots of ways the 70s was the fallout and the hangover
   from the 60s. I tell you, if ever I hear 'If you can remember
   the 60s you can't have been there' again I'll do my nut.
   Yeah yeah whatever, you old people were the first ever
   to have sex. Whatever. Stop going on about it. Which 70s
   icon and self-regarding prat died in his bathtub in Paris
   on 3 July 1971?

3 Politics in the 70s in Great Britain was hard going.
   It went ping pong backwards and forwards between
   Labour and the Tories. Tedious. Then Labour blew it as
   usual. Who announced his resignation on 16 March 1976?

4 Which bunch of total total nutters believed that 1975
   was the year that Armageddon would occur, the world
   would end, so they sold their homes and possessions to
   prepare for Jesus Christ's return to earth to establish the
   Kingdom of Heaven?

5 *Apollo 13* was the rocket that didn't make it to the
   moon. Jim Lovell was the captain, he must have been
   really pissed off as he'd already been on a previous trip
   where he'd been to the moon and not landed in *Apollo 8*.
   Unlucky bastard. When did *Apollo 13* launch?

Answers

1 It was Portugal. Personally I had no idea it was a democracy. Come on admit it, you're surprised too. Apparently the army got fed up with running the place. No surprise there.

2 Jim Morrison from the Doors. 'Break On Through To The Other Side' is a song all about following through. Not so cool and mysterious now is he?

3 Harold Wilson. He was a Labour Prime Minister who gave up because he realised he'd bitten off more than he could chew. As usual. Handed over to Jim Callaghan, who had bitten off more than he could chew.

4 Jehovah's Witnesses. What a bunch of donuts. Imagine being that stupid. As if the Kingdom of Heaven would involve them. Church of England only, pals, that's who Jesus is coming back for, if and when he makes his return.

5 11 April 1970. Splashed back down six days later. Very lucky. 'Houston, we have had a problem' is what they actually said, but in the film they used the misquote everyone knows because: a) filmmakers think their audiences are idiots who couldn't cope with hearing the right words and b) film audiences are idiots who couldn't cope with the right words.

The swinging 60s, ban the bomb, rise of feminism blah blah blah. The 60s was invented by the Beatles, everyone knows that, but other stuff did happen. So how much do you know about this decade? (No points for answering that . . .)

1 There's proof that there is definitely no God in the fact that he let Jane Fonda age. She got all nudey in the cult classic *Barbarella*, but in which year was the film released?

2 Flower power, like girl power, didn't achieve or solve anything. And besides, you can't run anything off a flower can you? Can you plug an iPod into a flower? No you can't. But who coined the phrase?

3 Computer games are for kids, grow up. The first one was invented by Steve 'Slug' Russell (grow up), Martin 'Shag' Graetz (grow up) and Wayne Wiitanen in 1962. What was it called?

4 As everyone knows, John 'JFK' Kennedy was the best-looking and youngest human man ever to be born. In which year did a sniper ruin those good looks by blowing his brains out?

5 The Rolling Stones are getting on a bit and at their age should know better. I don't know why they carry on touring, perhaps they're just really greedy? What was the title of their first album back in the 60s when they were good?

Answers

1 1968. While it has Jane Fonda in the buff, starkers, in the nude, in her birthday suit and with no clothes on, which is definitely a good thing, it was, however, where Duran Duran took their name from and it's for that reason I don't like it and nor should you.

2 Allen Ginsberg. What do you expect from a poet with a French name? Chancer.

3 Spacewar! Grow up.

4 1963. And no, I don't remember where I was when I heard that Kennedy had been killed, because I hadn't been born yet. Get over it bloke who remembers the 60s. I don't care. It's not interesting.

5 Released in 1964, it was unimaginatively called The Rolling Stones. Pull your finger out lads.

● ●

1 The Battle of Britpop was hardly the Beatles and the Rolling Stones was it? I mean come on, let's be honest. It involved Manc publican's friends Oasis and the other lot who thought they were commenting on Britain or something, yawn. Which Blur song went to number one in August 1995, beating boozehounds Oasis?

2 *The Sixth Sense* was that film with Bruce Willis where he's dead all the way through and if you know that before watching it, it really ruins it. Oh sorry, you haven't seen it. What is the famous line from the film?

3 John Major was the Prime Minister who liked peas, according to hit satire show *Spitting Image*. He also had a grey face according to that show too. And wore pants or something. No wonder no one took him seriously. Who was Chancellor of the Exchequer on Black Wednesday, 16 September 1992?

4 Telly Savalas popped his bald, shiny clogs on 22 January 1994. He was famous for being bald and sucking on lollipops. What is Telly short for? Clue: It's not Television.

5 Chess boffin Garry Kasparov was defeated in 1997 by a computer, signalling the end of man's reign over machine and to us being one step closer to *The Terminator* coming true. What was the computer called?

Answers

1 'Country House'.

2 'I see dead people.' Which means he can see Bruce Willis because Bruce Willis is dead. All the way through the film. That's the twist, but if you know that beforehand it's not so much of a twist at the end. It's like knowing *Planet of the Apes* is really Earth at the start. What you mean you haven't seen that either? Oh sorry.

3 It was Norman Lamont. The one who looked like a pissed-off badger. No one remembers him, apart from David Cameron who was one of his advisers, so he knows all about how to make the pound tank.

4 Aristotelis. Oh yeah, and also he used to say 'Who loves ya baby?', as well as the lollipops and the bald thing.

5 Deep Blue. Doesn't sound that scary, but trust me it's over, they're coming for us.

65 Music

1 Celebrity pin-cushion Pete Doherty used to be in a band called the Libertines before professionally dating Kate Moss. In which year did the first Libertines album get released?

2 I have mixed feelings about the Spice Girls. On the one hand they are credited with killing off Britpop, so thank you girls. On the other hand they didn't really replace it with much did they? That's not the question, obviously. The question is how many UK number one singles did they have?

3 Queen are, without doubt, the greatest rock band of all time and came from a time when men were man enough to wear leather caps. In which year did their seminal album *A Night at the Opera* come out?

4 Queen are, without doubt, the greatest rock band of all time. Their song 'Under Pressure' is a fine piece of work and the unofficial anthem for all bar staff working on Friday and Saturday nights. But who did they collaborate with on this track?

5 Song-singing, hip-swivelling, cheeseburger-chomping, spangly jumpsuit-wearing Elvis Presley played live in the UK on how many occasions?

Answers

1 2002.

2 Nine. Which I believe is the same number of people that bought Geri Halliwell's last album.

3 1975.

4 David Bowie.

5 None, never, not once. Yeah, same to you, Elvis.

66 More Pot Luck

Listen carefully! These questions could change your life! Ish.

1 The Sex Pistols changed the world with their brand of punk rock music. The world was never the same again. Everything was different is what bores tell us, but let's face it, that same year the Bee Gees were massive and George Michael flourishes despite being shit, basically. Poor old Johnny Rotten. How many studio albums did the Sex Pistols release?

2 Kerry Katona at one point was married to the most spud-faced member of Westlife. He's the one who left Westlife, but he left so long ago everyone's forgotten. In fact it's not like even the others in Westlife have noticed he's gone except they get to split the money four, not five ways. He didn't think it through. Who did Kerry used to be married to?

3 Phil 'Tuffers' 'The Cat' 'Two Sugars' Tufnell is a top bloke, down to earth, normal, a very handy spin bowler in his day. He used to wind up the England selectors, but I'd pick him every time, if only because he's a laugh and you'd be sure to shift some ales. From 1986 to 2002 which county side did he play for?

4 Busted were one of those bands that were designed to be hated by all sensible people, and fortunately didn't trouble the charts for long. No one knows what has happened to them all since, but one of them did marry Emma Griffiths, who is way above his average. Who is he?

5 Which TV show links these four: The Pistols, Kerry Katona, Tuffers and Emma Griffiths' husband?

Answers

1 One, *Never Mind the Bollocks, Here's the Sex Pistols*.
George Michael has released seven. Why on earth did
Johnny Rotten go into the jungle?

2 Brian McFadden. Jesus Christ. And to think she won *I'm
a Celebrity* ... I suppose it was all the Scousers voting
for her, otherwise you can't explain it.

3 Middlesex. He was a worthy winner in the jungle,
restoring a sense of reason to the whole thing.

4 Matt Willis. The lucky sod. Unbelievable that he won in
the jungle; also unbelievable he'd leave as top-flight a
woman as Emma unattended for three weeks.

5 It's *I'm a Celebrity* ... *Get Me Out of Here*! They've all
appeared on it. As the person reading the answers knows.
Keep up.

67 Sport: Football

Football was our idea and so even when we don't score as many goals as the other team, we still win as we invented the game and they wouldn't be there if it hadn't been for us.

1   There was nothing Godly about Diego Maradonna's handball in the 1986 World Cup quarter-final against England. In fact the phrase 'the hand of twat' has more of a resonance with that particular incident. What was the score after that little cheating fat bastard handballed the goal into the net?

2   Pele these days is more famous for a being a poster boy for erectile dysfunction (you'd keep that quiet, wouldn't you, no matter how much money they offered you?) He did, however, used to be quite a good footballer. How many World Cup medals did he win?

3   Boot-throwing, gum-chewing, racehorse-owning, cup-winning, red-faced manager Alex 'Fergie' Ferguson has won many trophies with Manchester United, but when did he join the club as manager?

4   Publican's friend Paul 'Gazza' Gascoigne was signed by an Italian team before quickly realising the beer there was served in metric volumes and that pints weren't available and returning home. What was the name of the club?

5   Which lingerie model, catwalk model and general all-round hottie goes out with the world's tallest man and England footballer Peter Crouch?

Answers

1 1-0. Little cheating fat bastard. He started it. What part of 'foot'ball did he not understand?

2 Three.

3 1986.

4 Lazio. I always loved Gazza, especially when he cried at the World Cup. Bless him. And there was the time at the FA Cup when he tried to kick himself in the face and popped his knee.

5 Abbey Clancy. May I just say Peter, you are batting well above your average there, pal.

68 Who Are You?

?

Another selection of chancers and knuckleheads for you.

1 Which Darren started off his career being hailed as the new Bobby Davro by Bob Monkhouse (what a kiss of death), then replaced Phillip Schofield in *Joseph and the Amazing Technicolor Dreamcoat*, baked a bun in Suzanne Shaw's oven and is now appearing on cruise ships and sleeping in his car?

2 Which irritating donut presented *Wacaday*, in which he waved around a giant foam hammer and wore stupid bright Hawaiian shirts and giant ridiculous glasses?

3 Which never-seen-ever-ever-ever-again-no-mark-chancer-who-the-hell-are-you-what's-your-name-again-we-haven't-heard-of-you-for-years-mate singer won the first ever UK version of *The X Factor*?

4 Spit the Dog was a puppet and couldn't move around by itself. Who was the beardy puppet master who has disappeared off the face of the earth and now owns his own candle business?

5 What was the showbiz name of spandex-covered, GMTV-exercise-section-presenting chancer, Derrick Evans?

Answers

1 Darren Day. Remember him? No me neither. His agent's forgotten who he is I reckon.

2 Timmy Mallett. Remember him? No me neither.

3 Steve Brookstein. Remember him? No me neither. He's probably joined the Foreign Legion or something to forget. Though to join the French Army you'd really have to want to forget, wouldn't you?

4 Bob Carolgees. Remember him? No me neither.

5 Mr Motivator. Remember him? No me neither.

69 Nature

We live in the natural world apparently; even those of us who live in blocks of flats are nothing in the face of nature. The planet could shrug and we'd all be gone, they say. And if you worry about that stuff you'll never get out of bed. It's not much of a surprise that nature is usually depicted as a woman now, is it? Capricious, powerful, answerable to no one.

1 Water features aren't the kind of thing the brewery will pay for in a beer garden. They're usually wrong but in this case they may well be right. I think it would just end up as a shower for the fox that craps in the sandpit and an outdoor toilet for when the gents is full. What is the tallest waterfall in the world?

2 Who I am? No not me, you know that. I thought I'd do this one like Henry Kelly used to do on *Going For Gold*, the Euro-humiliating quiz, by asking it like it's me. Anyway, carry on. Who am I? Measuring up to 108 feet, and weighing some 200 tons, I am a member of the Balaenopteridae family, live on krill, and am the largest animal known to have lived.

3 Australia is full of poisonous snakes, spiders, and strange creatures that have pockets for their keys. Kangaroos and wallabies are everywhere; they might be all symbolic of Australia but they're little more than giant jumping rats. It's an opinion. What is a young kangaroo called? (This is a question for the girls, they'll get this).

4 Hyenas laugh, or so they say. Though no one really knows if they're laughing at something or with something. Hard to tell. They're scavengers, and hang around waiting for a lion to finish whatever it was eating. Easy life, I reckon. They are, however, not dogs. Which mammals are they most closely related to?

5 If you were a Komodo dragon, you might be seriously pissed off. There can't be a day when a wildlife crew doesn't turn up and hang around watching your every move, as you eat, sleep, drink, crap, copulate, and all because you're a big lizard. Why Attenborough and the boys can't just hassle a cow or something for six months or so I don't know. At least British wildlife is a reasonable size and not all big. Where do Komodo dragons live?

Answers

1 The Angel Falls in Venezuela. They're 3212 feet high. I can't see the area manager approving anything like that in the beer garden in a hurry.

2 Blue whale. They've got a big fibreglass one in London at the Natural History Museum. Unfortunately it just hangs there like a giant moulding and doesn't wiggle its head in a jerky, stiff, unconvincing way like the animatronic dinosaurs down the corridor, so it's not half the draw they are.

3 It's a joey. Ahhhhh bless. They're still glorified rats in my view.

4 Meerkats and mongooses, for Pete's sake. No wonder they spend their time skulking around eating carrion and roadkill to try and act tough and get a bad reputation.

5 They live on the islands of Komodo, Rinca, Flores and Gili, Montang and Padar in Indonesia. If you said Komodo you are guessing, admit it.

70 British History: The 1600s

More British history. Get any of these wrong and hang your heads in shame.

1 Oliver Cromwell was Lord Protector, but he blew it because he banned Christmas. Mate, you went too far. But which illness killed him?

2 In 1688 the Glorious Revolution saw William and Mary installed on the English throne. It was called the Glorious Revolution because, unlike the French one, no one got hurt. No one. Not one person. Well, maybe a few, but we didn't go nuts like they did. But which king did they replace?

3 Guy Fawkes tried to blow up the Houses of Parliament on 5 November. He was doing it on behalf of Spain, which is hardly right. I mean, blow it up because you're pissed off about MPs' expense claims, but not because the Spanish told you to. But what was the year?

4 Queen Elizabeth I died in 1603. She had a hell of a track record – saw off the Spanish, gave Walter Raleigh the idea for the bike in return for him having invented potatoes and smoking. How many years was she on the throne?

5 What happened in Whitehall on 30 January 1649? And I won't accept smartarse answers like a pigeon flew past or something, we want proper big history here.

Answers

1 Malaria. Moral: don't fuck with Santa.

2 James II. No one remembers him.

3 1605

4 44 years.

5 The execution of King Charles I. Told you it was proper big history. He was a candle in the wind. Hang on, no he wasn't.

71 Famous People What I Have Met

I am, as you know, but a humbil publican. I have, however, had my own chat show and as a result encountered tons of famous people. And let me tell you, they are just like you and me: except for the big houses, expensive cars, holidays lasting at least six months, not having to pay for anything, queue-jumping and getting let off speeding fines by starstruck policemen, they are just like you and me.

1 The delectable Myleene Klass there (I'd delect her) and the best thing about this picture is, although I'm standing with two blokes, I'm not presented with much competition for Myleene; for obvious reasons. Two of the people in this picture were born in 1978, but which ones? I need both names for a point.

2 Look I didn't say I chose all the guests. Louis Walsh of course is one of the only people who can be both puppet master and muppet simultaneously. When he came on the show he said to me before the interview, 'Don't talk about the ting'. What was the thing I was not allowed to talk about?

3 Publican's friend Judy Finnigan and the not-wine-stealing Richard Madeley. What a lovely couple they were. What was the name of the ITV show they presented between 1988 and 2001?

4 Ah there she is, the lovely Holloughby Willoughby. Christ, it's been a year. Complete the name of the children's TV show she shot to fame in: '*Ministry of ...*'

5 Frankly though, I've saved the best until last (sorry Holloughby, but you did go and get married). Me and Brian May from Queen. What a top bloke he was. Who are the greatest rock band of all time?

Answers

1 Myleene Klass and Ricky 'The Hitman' Hatton. It has to be said, the years have been kinder to Myleene.

2 I don't know, he didn't tell me.

3 *This Morning*. They are sorely missed. Well, they were until Holloby Willoughby started presenting it. Schofield, the lucky, lucky bastard. Mind you, we still have to put up with Eamonn Holmes on Friday morning and let's be honest he's not much to look at is he?

4 Sadly it's *Ministry of Mayhem* and not *Ministry of Negligee*.

5 Queen, obviously. If you put anything else I'd give up now, you're not going to win.

72 The Theatre

Hands up who likes the theatre? Not that many of you, not since telly and the films came along. What's the point in the theatre when there's *Iron Man 2*? I rest my case. But still the theatre staggers on. Here's some more questions for you to scratch your heads at and wonder why.

1 Sir Laurence 'Larry' Olivier could be heard at the back of any theatre, and for that reason alone he's the greatest actor that ever lived. What's the point in all that mumbling you get nowadays eh? Which theatre was he the first artistic director of?

2 Bertolt Brecht was a German playwright whose plays are all miserable and weird. Stands to reason. I won't ask why, that's obvious. He had a big hit with *The Threepenny Opera*. It's the one with *Mack the Knife* in, that song they make bewildered kids sing on *The X Factor* every year on big-band night. Which English opera is *The Threepenny Opera* based on?

3 In which Shakespeare comedy is Lysander in love with Hermia who then falls in love with Demetrius who's in love with Helena, while all the while Titania … I can't be bothered. Side-splitting though, ooh my aching sides. Which play?

4 Willy Russell wrote *Entertaining Rita*, that one with Michael Caine in, which is great, because it's a movie so it spares you a trip to the theatre. He does have a long-running musical running in the West End, a tragic tale of Scousers. What's it called?

5 Andrew Lloyd Webber is a nexus of mystery. Standing atop a pile of cash generated by *Joseph and the Amazing Technicolor Dreamcoat*, he dominates Britain's theatrical

landscape. One day people will talk of him in the same awed tones as they do of Shakespeare. Possibly. What was the name of his unstoppable improbable hit based around words by miserable poet T.S. Eliot?

Answers

1 The National Theatre. That's the one on the river I've never been to. And nor have you.

2 *The Beggar's Opera*. Me neither. No one's seen either of them. Ever. Let alone both.

3 *A Midsummer Night's Dream*. There's a bloke in it called Bottom. Shakespeare's the greatest playwright the world has ever seen.

4 *Blood Brothers*. They need to make a film of it and they can stop.

5 *Cats*. At one point in the eighties everyone in the UK had seen it. Dark days indeed.

73 Science and Technology

We live in an age of sci-tech – yes, I said sci-tech – and you can't move for some amazing gadget or app – yes, I said app – to help solve problems you never knew you had. If I was a prick, I'd say the machines are taking over and we are going to be replaced by robots, but I'm not a prick, and that won't happen. Grow up.

1 Computers – no one knows how computers actually work, at least the people who ought to know, e.g. the hopeless drongos in PC World. Stone me, what a bunch of useless bastards. Ask them this one and they won't know it. What does the M in IBM stand for?

2 My favourite bridge is the Forth Railway Bridge. Red, made of iron, connecting bits of Scotland – it doesn't muck about. But this isn't a question about the Forth Railway Bridge, it's a question about another bridge. When it was opened in 1981, what was the world's longest single-span suspension bridge?

3 There's a hole in the ozone layer that will kill us all by 1980, according to scientists from the seventies. Ah well, never mind. Who'd want to be proved right about a thing like that? But the hole that destroyed the world in 1980 was made by CFCs. What does CFC stand for?

4 In the periodic table – remember that? Me either – which element has the symbol K?

5 Nicholas Copernicus was the first man to successfully postulate a heliocentric cosmology – which to you and me means he figured out that the sun was the centre of the solar system, not the earth – and for his trouble the Pope threw him out the Church. Perhaps he'd have been better off molesting kids. Anyway, where was Copernicus from?

Answers

1 Machines. Obvious when you think about it. The B stands for business, the I – leaving that one to you to guess.

2 The Humber Bridge. Connecting Hull to nowhere, which is ironic seeing as Hull pretty much is nowhere, but they could hardly connect it to itself.

3 Chlorofluorocarbons. Catchy.

4 It's potassium, believe it or not. God knows what chemicals the bloke who compiled that was on. It's not even close.

5 He was Polish. Yeah, I know.

The 60s are the decade when everyone let their hair down and we lost the plot and an empire as a direct result. I blame Paul McCartney for everything that has gone wrong in this country. I hold him personally responsible.

1 The 60s was the time of the Cold War, when the Americans were paranoid about the Russians being paranoid about the Americans being paranoid about the Russians being paranoid about the Americans. In order to feel less paranoid about each other they tooled up with loads of nukes and heaped tons of shit on each other every other day. What was the name of the pilot of the U2 spy plane that was shot down in 1960?

2 Sean Connery was the best Bond by a mile, no dispute. Anyone who disagrees can leave now. All the stuff we think of as Bond started under him: the gadgets, the cars, the women, the suit, the gambling etc. All the films after that have been lame. No argument. Shut it. The second Bond film was released in 1963: what is its title?

3 British music is the best and it was never better than during the 60s or during any time Queen were playing. Most music nowadays is a direct result of British music from the 60s. Don't argue. Which 1964 number one hit record by the Kinks is commonly regarded as being the first hard-rock hit and the beginnings of heavy metal?

4 On 26 July 1965 the Maldives – never been there, I hear it's very pleasant for somewhere overseas – gained their independence from whom?

5 The 60s were all about bright ideas and new ways of doing things, and the people who were around at the time still crap on about it. However, most of it was filmed in black and white so it looks almost as long ago as the war. Shut up Grandpa. One of those bright ideas was new towns and cities. Which new town was founded on 23 January 1967?

Answers

1 Gary Powers. It is not on record what he thinks of Bono and his mates. It's just a shame the Russians didn't shoot those four chancers down.

2 *From Russia With Love*. It's the one where he beats a bloke up on a train. Big finish or what?

3 'You Really Got Me'. If you said 'Waterloo Sunset' you need your head examined. Or 'Plastic Man'. Or 'Sunny Afternoon'.

4 Great Britain. Their loss. Then again, right now they could be somewhere to send anyone who breaks the conditions of their ASBO. We didn't think it through.

5 Milton Keynes. So it's really old, even though it's a new town. So whenever they brag about how up-to-date the place is, remember it's in its mid-forties and has got a paunch.

75 Sport: The Ashes

The Ashes is the greatest sporting rivalry in all history – no one can deny that it matters more than any other cricketing trophy. Winning the Ashes reflects honourably on the team that wins, and showers defeat on the loser. Here's twelve questions in a special one-off round to see if you know your cricket.

1 Who held the Ashes from 1882-1892?

2 Who held the Ashes from 1893-1896?

3 Who held the Ashes from 1903-1905?

4 Who held the Ashes from 1911-1912?

5 Who held the Ashes from 1926-1929?

6 Who held the Ashes from 1932-1933?

7 Who held the Ashes from 1953-1956?

8 Who held the Ashes from 1970-1972?

9 Who held the Ashes from 1977-1981?

10 Who held the Ashes from 1986-1987?

11 Who held the Ashes in 2005?

12 And finally, who held the Ashes from 2010?

Answers

1 England.

2 England.

3 England.

4 England.

5 England.

6 England.

7 England.

8 England.

9 England.

10 England.

11 England.

12 England.

76 Comedy

It is well known that the British have the greatest sense of humour in the world. Otherwise we wouldn't have got *Fawlty Towers* would we? No, God would have given it to the Germans, wouldn't he? Mind you, it's the loneliest, bravest, most difficult job in the world[*] and they all want to top themselves, so it's not a barrel of laughs providing laughs. Let's see what you know about the greatest laughter makers in the world.

1 *The Two Ronnies* – classic stuff, four candles, brilliant, because it sounds like fork handles you see, but he's asking for four candles, simply brilliant – played private investigators. What were they called?

2 Russ Abbot was huge way back when with his *Madhouse*. Priceless stuff, just hilarious. Basildon Bond who was sort of like James Bond, and that jock he did. Top-notch stuff. Priceless. They don't do stuff like that any more. What instrument did Russ Abbot play when he was in the Black Abbots?

3 Sid James – wa ha ha ha ha ha – that was his catchphrase, hard to put across on the page, that, but there we go. He was great. Everyone remembers him from the *Carry On* films, of course, but whose sitcom flatmate was he?

4 Arthur Askey is one of those comedians from way back who you're meant to like, even though his act seemed to mainly consist of him shouting stuff in a music hall that you can't understand now without a history degree or a 1936 almanac to know what he's going on about (though

---

[*] That's what all the papers tell us. And it must be even more difficult now they're not allowed to push the boundaries any more in an edgy exciting way blah blah.

I reckon that applies to all comics). What was his famous catchphrase?

5 Spike Milligan was the bloke who invented all the modern comedy you see now. The whole lot, everyone owes him big time. Half of them know it and have a guilty aspect as a result, the rest don't and should be ashamed of themselves. BUT! Spike was his nickname: what was his real first name?

(Answers on page 174)

Go on, you can fit another one in before the end . . .

Towards the End of the Night

You're an hour and half into the quiz. It started late because the quizmaster's Allegro broke down and his TomTom doesn't have the right postcode in it (mind you, he's been drinking in this place for fourteen years so he should know where it is, but his box of questions and the PA he brings with him are too heavy to carry on the bus). With the delay, you've found yourself quaffing a couple more pints of export than you planned to. This meant you missed two questions in the music round because your bladder isn't what it was, and these last couple of rounds are now crucial. It doesn't help that the sports round has already happened and you didn't hear the third from last question. This stage of the evening is when the quiz can be won or lost, when you can stare into the quiz abyss or take your rightful place on the podium and clutch that frozen chicken to your bosom with pride. So, make sure you dig deep into your brain and find the answers that you need. A pub quiz is a marathon, not a sprint (though unlike both a marathon and a sprint, it requires no physical effort of any kind). The hard yards are yet to come. Pull yourself together, focus. Guts, grit, determination, bladder control. Get stuck in.

Answers

1 Charley Farley and Piggy Malone. Classic, priceless stuff.

2 The drums.

3 Tony Hancock in *Hancock's Half Hour*.

4 'Hello Playmates!' Yeah. Me either.

5 Terry.

77 Compulsory Literary Round

More questions on books for the publishers. I reckon they want some stuff they know the answers to so they can win this quiz and look big in front of their friends.

1 The *Chronicles of Narnia* films didn't do that well*, but they still made them into books. There are seven books in the series; name them all for one point.

2 Shane 'The Legend' Richie** is many things, one of which is the author of his autobiography. Can you tell me the natty and hilarious title of this book please?

3 No one who has read Shakespeare has ever really enjoyed it. He clearly couldn't stand writing the stuff either. People who say they like it don't really, they're just saying they do. What is the name of King's Lear's eldest daughter in the tragedy *King Lear*?

4 *Animal Farm*, no not that one, get your mind out of the gutter and back in the pub. George Orwell's *Animal Farm* was set on which fictional farm?

5 George Orwell also wrote the literary classic *1984*. In which year was this book set?

---

* Come off it, a talking lion. Grow up. Hobbits are much more believable.
** Another mention for you Shane.

Answers

1   *The Lion, the Witch and the Wardrobe*; *Prince Caspian:
    The Return to Narnia*; *The Voyage of the Dawn Treader*;
    The Silver Chair; *The Horse and His Boy*; *The Magician's
    Nephew* and *The Last Battle*. Deduct points if you like
    them.

2   *Rags To Richie – The Story So Far*. Do you get it? Because
    his name is Shane Richie and it's like that rags to riches
    phrase, but instead he's used his name because it sounds
    like it. Brilliant.

3   Goneril. Oof sounds nasty, you can probably get a cream
    for that. You don't need to read *King Lear*, you know
    what's going to happen by the way Shakespeare calls it a
    tragedy. Clue's in the name, they all die.

4   Manor Farm. Of course, classic book with great
    characters such as Squealer and Pinkeye. Oi what did I
    tell you, get your filthy mind back in the pub.

5   1984. Mind you, it might be a great book, but he's still
    to blame for *Big Brother*. Nice one George, thanks a lot.
    Although in his version of *Big Brother*, dreadful as it
    was, it was for people's own good.

78 Drums, Drummers and Drumming

Drums are the best instrument to play because you can do a lot of it one-handed whilst supping from a refreshment, maybe of the booze variety, and no one will care. Leave your pint on the floor tom, it's like a coffee table really – just don't forget it's there or you'll knock it over. Paradiddles at the ready!

1 Buddy Rich was a phenomenal drummer, easily the greatest drummer the world has ever seen. Who defeated him in a drum duel on TV in 1978?

2 Sting, eh? How did that happen? 'Rooooooooooooox-anne' etc. Well I'll tell you how that happened – he had an amazing drummer sat right behind him, driving the whole thing along and making it sound fabulous. Who was the drummer in The Police?

3 What do the Eagles, the Dave Clark Five, Genesis, the Carpenters and the Monkees all have in common?

4 Oasis were without a doubt one of the classic bands – their music has filled pubs night after night up and down the land. Though if I hear 'Wonderwall' again I swear to God I won't be able to account for my actions. How many drummers have there been in Oasis – to date? And who are they?

5 Adam and the Ants were bonkers – when you stop to take a look at them you wonder what in God's name anyone liked about them. Well, it wasn't Adam – he was totally out there; it wasn't the songs, they were mental; no, it was the drumming. Why?

Answers

1   Animal on *The Muppet Show*.

2   Stewart Copeland. He couldn't stand Sting either. Top bloke.

3   Singing drummers. Don, Dave, Phil, Karen and Mickey all sang. Karen was pretty good too.

4   Four. Tony McCarroll, Alan White, Zak Starkey and Chris Sharrock. A high rate of drumming attrition.

5   There were two drummers! Altogether now: Bur rumba bumba bumba rumba bumba bumba dum dum. Bur rumba bumba bumba rumba bumba bumba dum dum.

79 Sport: the Olympics

The pinnacle of sporting competition, the Olympics is the world's greatest sportsmen and women joining together to see who is the greatest in the world. And every time Britain makes a token effort, picks up a couple of medals, and proves that taking part is much a more dignified way to behave than the Americans' vulgar scramble for medals.

1 The 2012 Olympics is going to be held in London. Let's face it; it's going to be a bit shit, isn't it? I mean, it's never going to be as good as the one in China with their beautiful stadiums built by the billion slave labourers they have to hand. When was the last time London made a complete hash of the Olympics by hosting it?

2 The Americans frankly win every bloody medal going unless Usain Bolt is in the race. One year they gave everybody else a chance and didn't turn up. Which year was this?

3 Cheating Canadian bastard Ben Johnson got the gold medal in the 100m race, only to have it taken away after he failed the drug test. Name the year and city of this incident.

4 Daley Thompson is one of our greatest Olympic competitors, what a bloke – winning the decathlon shows that you can be the jack and the master of all. How many decathlon gold medals did he win?

5 One sport that is sadly missing from the Olympic Games is the tug-o-war. Frankly I'd much rather see this on the telly than archery and dressage. When was this fine activity last in the Olympic Games?

Answers

1 1948. It was supposed to be in 1944, but got cancelled because of the war. Nice one, thanks a lot, Adolf. Incidentally the Germans hosted it in Berlin in 1936 before the war. So they basically waited until just after they got to hold the games, and then started a war* so no one else could have a go. Bastards.

2 1980. The Americans boycotted the 1980 Moscow Olympics in protest at the Soviet invasion of Afghanistan (ooh the irony).

3 Seoul, 1988. Cheating Canadian bastard. Linford got silver, great bloke.

4 Two! They were in 1980 and 1984. This has nothing to do with the fact that the Americans weren't there in 1980 and the Russians weren't present in 1984, nothing to do with that at all.

5 1920. Now you if you want to see the tug-o-war you have to watch *The World's Strongest Man*. Bank Holidays can last for ever.

---

* They started it.

80 Before They Were Famous

All famous people are worthless layabouts. There I've said it. Jonathan Ross? He wouldn't lend you so much as a cup of sugar. Jamiroquai? He wouldn't lend you his mobile to call your mum if she was sick. Chris Evans? He'd sooner lie in a bath of champagne all day than lift a finger for anyone else. Michael Parkinson? Wouldn't piss on you if you were on fire. I don't know any of this for sure, and have selected these celebrities at random but, I mean, they're all the same (well except any member of Queen, of course). Many of them have claimed to have done a trial for a football club in order to seem interesting and cool, but lots of famous people had other jobs before they were famous.

1   Fake Scot and self-professed football nut, feather-cut proto-mullet pioneer, multiple-blonde-squiring Rod 'The Mod' Stewart was what before music intervened?

2   Jack White from the White Stripes – and let's get this straight, they really need a bass player; Chas and Dave are piano, bass and drums, I mean, be reasonable – wasn't always a ground-breaking wailing axe-man. Before he became a top-notch rock and pop star what did he do? You won't get it, you don't stand a chance.

3   Girls Aloud. Oof. They've done well haven't they? I don't think anyone imagined they'd still be going now, but they get bigger and better and oh my God Cheryl Cole oof. What did four out of five of them do before they shot to fame via *Popstars: The Rivals*?

4   Ozzy Osbourne eh? Star of *The Osbournes* – he got that job because of his name. What a character, eh? That man has been around the block, he has done the lot, and married to Sharon Osbourne too. It's a wonder he's still with us. What did he do before he was plucked from obscurity and shot to fame?

5 Sting eh? God help us all. Bryan Ferry. Gawd. Chris Tarrant – top bloke. What jobs did these three have before they became idle and famous?

Answers

1 He was a gravedigger. Which is odd as he does give the impression of never having done a day's work in his life – with all due respect, belting out 'Sailing' can't really be classed as work.

2 He was an upholsterer.

3 Waitresses. Only Nadine hadn't been a waitress. She just did talent shows till she got picked. Never done a day's work in her life.

4 He worked in an abattoir. What better preparation could there be for winding up in *The Osbournes*?

5 Teachers. I suppose the best way to look at that is Sting isn't teaching any more.

81 Chatshow Hosts

Chatshow hosts are a special breed – they ask the sorts of questions publicists demand their guests be asked.

1 Shell-shocked chat show veteran Michael 'Parky' Parkinson interviewed Muhammad Ali once, don't you know, but doesn't really like to talk about it much. Which guest appeared on *Parkinson* the most?

2 Sir Terry Wogan, famous for *Children in Need* and making the unbearable *Eurovision Song Contest* not fully bearable but a bit more bearable, also had a chat show on BBC1. Which TV madman claimed to be the son of God on *Wogan*?

3 Alan Titchmarsh used to be famous for a gardening programme with that annoying cockney bloke and the ginger girl deficient in the bra department. What was this show called? Clue: it's not *Gardeners' World*.

4 Michael Aspel, who is a sort of Michael Parkinson-lite for daytime television, first shot to fame on *Come Dancing* and *Crackerjack*. He used to have his own chatshow but what was it called?

5 David Dickinson was the first chatshow host ever to be made entirely out of mahogany and the first antiques dealer to accidentally sell himself at auction. Complete his never-tiresome catchphrase: 'As cheap as …'

Answers

1 Beard-growing, motor-trike-riding, knob-flashing Billy Connolly. He appeared fifteen times.

2 David Icke. Poor sod.

3 *Ground Force*. Haha *Ground Force*, see what they did there because they're digging in the ground, that's priceless, I love it.

4 *Aspel And Company*. Sounds more like a solicitors' firm than a chatshow.

5 'chips'. I would have accepted 'daytime television' too.

The 90s might not seem that long ago, but really what that means is you're getting old. Pull yourself together. John Major was Prime Minister twenty years ago. Yeah! Shit!

1 *Titanic* is one of those films where the bad guys are all British. Even the iceberg went to Eton. When you stop and think about it the film isn't much cop – you know the ending, and Leonardo Di Whatsit is a pipsqueak. I'm being polite. 'I'm the king of the world!' No you're not, you're a bloke in a flat cap. Anyway, how many Oscars did it win in 1998?

2 The Millennium was a total fiasco. What a joke. The Dome. The Queen's face when she had to hold Tony Blair's hand and sing 'Auld Lang Syne'. Concorde flying through the gloom and no one seeing it. The attempt to set fire to a river. When Prince sang 'Tonight I'm going to party like it's 1999', he didn't have any of that useless twaddle in mind. This country's fucked and has been for at least a decade. What is the Dome now known as?

3 *Doctor Who* made an abortive comeback attempt with one of Mrs McGann's boys giving it a go. It was set in America, so was obviously never going to work. The episode itself was set in 1999, but what year did it air, only to never see the light of day again until the shouty northern bloke came along?

4 Barings Bank collapsed in 1995, money swirling down the plughole, never to be seen again, and after it happened everyone said 'Oh well that won't happen again, the banks will behave themselves'. Hmmmm. What was the name of the banker who broke the bank?

5 The big music movement from America was grunge.
A bunch of scruffy lads acted like they'd invented
the idea of turning up their guitars loud and singing
unhappily about stuff, even though they were ripping
off British punk, which in turn was reacting to Queen's
brilliance and dominance of all music forms. So without
Freddie, Brian, Roger and John, no Kurt. Remember that.
Who is the drummer from Nirvana who has gone on to
have chart success with Foo Fighters?

Answers

1 11. Incredible isn't it? 'I'm the king of the world!' Shut it.

2 It's the O2. A big proper venue that really you ought to
play at least twice to get a feel of the place.

3 1996. Nerds should know that one. If they get it wrong
they're expecting you to give them a dead arm now,
which is the nerd equivalent of the Vulcan nerve pinch
they like so much in *Star Trek*.

4 Nick Leeson. He lost £827 million. Poor bastard. Now,
I've had slow weekends in my time where I end up
behind on snacks, but I've never sweated that kind of
money out of my behind.

5 Dave Grohl. He's good, but let's face it, he's no Roger
Taylor.

83 Art: More Art

1 *Sunflowers*, the classic painting by Vincent Van Gogh, is part of a series of paintings he knocked out after he accidently over-ordered on a trade amount of yellow paint and realised he could paint sunflowers. The sunflower is the state flower of which American state?

2 Whistler's most well known painting was *Whistler's Mother* or *Arrangement in Grey and Black: The Artist's Mother*, as the art boffins will have you call it. If you've seen it, the old dear looks a miserable sort, doesn't she? And she's not even bothering to look at her son while he paints her. Still thank God he didn't ask her if she'd mind going nude, he'd have been giving himself clues. What was Whistler's first name?

3 Andy Warhol was a timewaster. He spent his time painting soup cans when he could have painted beers cans. Total charlatan. I'd like to have shot Andy Warhol, but someone beat me to it. In which year did he die?

4 Even evil dictators have favourite artists and Adolf Hitler was no different. It's said he even took inspiration for his look from a painting called *Lucifer* by this artist. But what was his name?

5 *The South Bank Show*, *Imagine* and *The Culture Show* are all examples of art programming on television. If you ask me, you can forget all those as the best one was *Art Attack*. Who presented this show during its run between 1990 and 2007?

Answers

1 Kansas. Easy, everyone knows the state flowers of the US. Come on, try harder.

2 James. American-born, but British-based. Typical, coming over here, using our paints.

3 1987. What a timewaster, he didn't even paint Heinz cans.

4 Franz Von Stuck. German. If anyone knows what the devil looks like, it's definitely going to be a German bloke isn't it?

ANSWER Yes.

5 Neil Buchanan. Me neither.

84 Pot Luck

Yet another round of random questions, maybe even creating the impression that at this late stage the quiz is losing all shape and form, aside from momentum. But you're so pissed now it doesn't matter. Answer these random things if you can.

1 Trainspotting used to be what nerds did before the internet came along and saved them the bother of having to leave the house. Tragic in a way, there was something noble about the trainspotter: alone, pitted against the elements, looking for that one last locomotive, and no chance of accidentally browsing for porn. Mecca for the trainspotter is the National Railway Museum – where?

2 Poker is very fashionable now, isn't it? Everyone likes poker. Well they say they do. Poker blah blah! Texas Hold 'Em blah blah! Who cares? I don't, I shall not follow the herd on that one. What is the maximum number of players in a game of poker?

3 Scotland – not been many questions about Scotland in this book so far, so to shore up Scottish sales here's one. That should cover it. What might you hope to see if you were visiting Drumnadrochit?

4 In this country the Prime Minister is just that, the Queen's first minister, as she is the head of state. It's the perfect system and, as well as being the best in the world, it also nets us millions in tourism every year as foreign schoolchildren come to gawp at Buckingham Palace and stand in groups at the entrances to tube stations, the stupid fuckers. In France, where they haven't thought it through, they have a president – how long is a presidential term?

5 Who had a hit in the 1980s with 'A Good Heart'? And an extra point if you can tell me which band he sang with before his solo career.

Answers

1 York. Worth a visit if you're an old-school nerd. They've probably all settled down and had kids by now that lot and turned their backs on the locos. It's all sad, that's the truth.

2 It's eight apparently. Not that I care.

3 The Loch Ness Monster. To which I say, grow up! Snap out of it! It's for kids.

4 Five years.

5 Feargal Sharkey. And he sang with the Undertones. They were really good.

85 Nature

The natural world is such an amazing thing that if you stopped to think about all the beetles and bugs and insects, you might start to whimper and shiver like a beaten dog. Well, snap out of it, grow up. We invented DDT, we are their masters!! And as their masters we know about them, and they know nothing about us!!

1 Spiders: girls don't like them and they don't even know why they don't like them. They just don't. Maybe they don't like them so that men have something to do in these barren, grey, tawdry, gender-role-devoid times. Thanks girls. What is the name of the largest spider? Not his name, as in Geoff, its species' name.

2 Pelicans have those great big bills – not like MPs for expenses (bit of satire there), for catching fish. There was that film too, called *The Pelican Brief*, which was not about a pelican's underpants – there's no way Denzel Washington would appear in something that stupid. The largest is the Dalmatian Pelican – how wide are its wings?

3 Africa is full of amazing animals that were at one point regarded as monsters and freaks. Compare an elephant to a squirrel or a badger and, well, the thing is odd-looking innit? These animals couldn't be explained, they were too fantastic. Which African animal was named a camelopard because no one knew what the hell it was?

4 I love pigs. In India the cow is sacred, but I truly believe we should worship pigs. Any animal that can lay down its life to deliver up such delights as chops, bacon, gammon, ham, sausages, pork belly, salami, pepperami, knuckle, spare ribs, ribs and, above all, pork scratchings should be worshipped, honoured and loved. And if it wants to wallow in muck, fair play. It's doing its bit. But why do pigs like to wallow in muck?

5 Animals have the normal names we use and they also have Latin names that biologists use in order to make themselves appear more interesting. What is the species name for the Westland Lowland Gorilla? And it's not *westlandus lowlandus gorilla*. Guess again.

Answers

1 It's called a Goliath birdeater. Only one of them has ever been seen eating a bird, but that's how reputations get going. They're a kind of tarantula but I wanted the species name, I'm afraid.

2 Ten feet. Yes ten feet. Huge. If anyone answered in metric, three metres, house rules dictate that you score no more points in this round. You'd never get one of those on the barbie would you? And they'd probably taste all fishy.

3 The giraffe. Folks back then thought it was sort of half camel, half leopard. It isn't obviously, it's a great big neck. With legs. That's like calling an elephant a rhinosnakeface. Stupid.

4 They don't have sweat glands. They can't sweat, so it's the only way they can cool off properly. Someone bung 'em a pint. In fact the least any of us can do is buy a pig a pint.

5 It's *Gorilla gorilla gorilla*. Another hard day at the species office there. That one's a proper Friday lunchtime can't-we-just-go-to-the-pub? name.

86 Prohibition

The Americans once banned booze*. Yes, that's right. If you ever need more evidence that the Yanks never had a plot to lose, that's it. They banned booze from top to bottom, and they did it to make people's lives better. Mental, mental, mental. They even called it 'The Noble Experiment', which just shows how mental they were. These questions may or may not be ones you can answer, but they offer a glimpse into the American mind ...

1 When did Prohibition run from and until?

2 Al Capone was a notorious gangster in the eyes of some, a public-spirited hero who supplied booze to a thirsty nation in the eyes of others. I'll let you decide which one he was, we're all grown ups here. What was Al short for?

3 Which sport grew up as a result of bootleggers needing to transport their stock around the country quickly?

4 Where did you have to go if you wanted a drink, seeing as all the bars were closed?

5 When Prohibition was partly repealed by the signing of an amendment to the original Act in March 1933, who said 'I think this would be a good time for a beer'?

---

* Though they didn't think it through and didn't ban the consumption of booze: you couldn't buy it, or sell it, but you could drink it. Idiots.

Answers

1 1920 to 1933 (and longer in some states). Thirteen years. Jesus. I mean I once went a week without because I was put on antibiotics and the doc said no, but thirteen years? By the end of that week I was climbing the walls. Is it any coincidence that during that time the US economy suffered the Great Depression?

2 Alphonse.

3 Stock car racing. You'd take a 'stock-looking' car and customise it to outrun the police. Amazing the things people will do for booze.

4 A speakeasy. By the end of the 1920s there were 10,000 speakeasies in Chicago and Al Capone controlled them all. I wonder if he made them do theme nights?

5 President Franklin D. 'FDR' R. Roosevelt. But sadly there wasn't any. He didn't think it through.

87 Famous People What I Have Met

My life has been mainly one of pouring pints and lunching ploughmen, but by an extraordinary quirk of fate and chance I have found myself rubbing shoulders with what are commonly known as celebrities. The word 'celebrity' somehow implies that there is something to celebrate about these people, but believe me, there ain't. But you wouldn't sell many issues of *Heat* if you had 'This Week's Lowlife Chancer Sponger News!' on the cover.

1 Here I am being clonked righteously by Ricky 'The Hitman' Hatton. Actually it's unfair to class him as a celebrity seeing as he actually does something, and something pretty dangerous. We met in early 2008 – who had he just fought for the WBC Welterweight Championship?

2 Konnie Huq was the longest serving female presenter of what? (To be honest you all know, I just wanted to show you a picture of me and Konnie. She's lovely.)

3 Here you see me with Yorkshire TV celebrity chef James Martin. He likes puddings and Ferraris, apparently. What is the name of the show he presents on Saturday mornings that is set in a kitchen? You know, the one with the omelette thing like it's *Top Gear* for food. Which it isn't.

4 Help me. Who is this man? And what does he do?

5 Here he is, little Ron Weasley from the old Potter movies. He's minted, doesn't need to work ever again. Bastard. Though it feels odd saying that because you think of him as a kid from the films. He's not though, so I'll say it like it is – bastard. What's his real name, and for a bonus point, what vehicle did he buy to amuse himself?

Answers

1 Floyd Mayweather. Down in the tenth. But he's more use to you in a fight than any member of the cast of *Hollyoaks*.

2 *Blue Peter*.

3 *Saturday Kitchen*. Come on, I gave you that one.

4 It's Jason Gardiner. He's a judge on *Dancing on Ice*. I am on red alert in this picture as well you can see.

5 Rupert Grint. And he bought an ice cream van – just because he could. Imagine. I mean, I'd buy a carvery if I could, but no, I can't afford one. No, and the brewery don't care, or the pub management corporation … All I want is a selection of hot meats laid out for punter perusal, is that too much to ask? With a little basket of mustard blister packs? Come on.

88 TV Detectives

Everyone loves a TV detective apart from, obviously, a TV criminal. There's been loads of them, in fact there's been too many and I don't reckon they should make more until we've had a chance to watch all the ones they've already made. Let's see how much you know about them.

1 The only thing that anyone remembers about *Van Der Valk* is the theme tune. Altogether now, ba ba baa ba ba baa ba ba ba ba ba ba baa, ba ba baa babababab baa. It's a classic. A well-known British crooner did a vocal version of the song called 'And You Smiled'. But who was it?

2 No one has a name in real life like Remington Steele, no one, not unless you're a razor. Still, Pierce Brosnan is a pretty unbelievable name too. In which year was *Remington Steele* first broadcast in the US?

3 Starting in 1989, Belgian moustache-sporting TV detective Hercule Poirot was played by which David in the ITV series *Agatha Christie's Poirot*?

4 *Z Cars* was the first TV drama to try to honestly portray the police blah blah blah, get over it. Who played PC 'Fancy' Smith in the series?

5 The Sweeney, The Sweeney la la la laaa la la la la, The Sweeney, The Sweeney la la la laaa la la la la. Yeah anyway *The Sweeney* was that show with Morse and the bloke from *Minder* in it. Great times. 'You're nicked you slag.' Great stuff. Morse played a character called Regan but what was the name of the character that the bloke from *Minder* played?

Answers

1 Matt Monro. For those youngsters out there who don't
   know either of those references, it's a bit like Robbie
   Williams making up words to the theme tune of *The Bill*.
   That doesn't bear thinking about.

2 1982. Mind you, the *Mary Rose* was raised, Channel 4
   started and the Falklands war began that year, so you
   can't be blamed for not remembering that. It's low on the
   list of important happenings.

3 Suchet. You know the bloke in that diabolical Jason
   Statham film *The Bank Job*. If you've not seen it, don't
   bother, you'll never get that time back. I had to watch it
   because I was meant to be interviewing Jason Statham
   and then the bastard pulled out. What a terrible waste
   of time. If he'd turned up I'd have been able to tell him
   what I thought of the film.

4 Brian Blessed. Well he had to get his foot on the acting
   ladder somehow.

5 George Carter. That's not Carter from *Get Carter*, he was
   played by Alfie from *Zulu*.

89 Sayings

More sayings, bon mots*, old wives' whatevers. You really should know these, even to rule them out.

1 Everyone knows this one: 'An Englishman's home is ...'

2 Sayings about animals now. 'A cat has ...'

3 More home stuff for you all now. 'Home is ...'

4 This next one is the bane of every child's life come Christmas, and one I've never quite got my head round. 'It's better to give ...'

5 And finally, medicine: 'Blood is ...'

---

* French words.

Answers

1 An Englishman's home is his castle.' This is only true if he lives in a castle, which does not apply to many. I live in a pub, a lot of people I know live in houses (and they're mortgaged up to the eyeballs, poor sods) and one of my regulars, Bob the Log, lives in the bins over by Tesco, so this doesn't work for any of us.

2 'A cat has nine lives.' You try telling that to the one I hit the other day in the Daimler Sovereign on the way back from the cash and carry. Christ what a mess. Mind you, I'm a dog person, so too bad, them's the breaks.

3 'Home is where the heart is.' Yeah, is that so? Well then, what about Tony Bennett? He left his in San Francisco. And Paul Young's home is wherever he lays his hat. Think it through lads.

4 'It's better to give than to receive.' Oh come on! When has that ever been true? Well, OK, apart from in prison.

5 'Blood is thicker than water.' Whoever came up with that nonsense had clearly never met a haemophiliac, or seen ice.

90 Who's Who?

More names that aren't real names for you now. Hopefully now 'Doctor Who' as the answer to these questions is a dim and distant memory.

1 Who is Bobby Davro? Now, I'm not the first person to have said that, and Lord knows I won't be the last, but it's not his real name, probably to protect his family. So, what is Bobby Davro's real name?

2 He was the second man on the moon, though really they landed at the same time, so to make a big deal of it might start to get on his wick some forty years later, but what is Buzz Aldrin's real first name?

3 Slash – from Guns N Roses and other bands that won't get on my jukebox – obviously uses a stage name. Though one wonders if he knows what it means in this country. Probably not. Though I expect by now someone has filled him in on that. But what is Slash's* real name?

4 Who the hell is Mary Isobel Catherine Bernadette O'Brien? Me, I don't know. I mean I've got the answers and I look and I think naaaaaaaaaaah.

5 Sting is many things, and you can all judge him for yourselves. He's an easy target frankly, he's bloody fish in a barrel. What a Herbert. But he has a real name, which presumably wasn't pretentious enough (see, easy). What is it?

---

* Tee hee.

Answers

1 Robert Nankeville.

2 It's Buzz. He changed it by deed poll in the early 1980s. Sorry about that.

3 Saul Hudson.

4 Dusty Springfield. How do you get Dusty Springfield out of that lot?

5 Gordon Sumner. Ponce.

91 Pictures!

Also known as the 'What the hell is that?' round

• •

The human eye can play tricks on us, as we all know, especially when wearing beer goggles*. Some images can play with your perception – you know the one, is it a candlestick, or just two faces opposite each other? But every now and then you see something that your brain simply can't take in or identify. So, it's time for the pictures round, also known as the 'What the hell is that?' round.

1   What the hell is that?

---

* There really is no need for me to explain to you what beer goggles are. If you don't know by now, you never will.

2 What's the hell is this?

3 What the hell is this?

4 What the hell is this?

5 What the hell is this?

Answers

1 It's a naked mole rat. For all your staring, no one's has eyes, ears and teeth.

2 It's the Paris Gun. The Germans used it to shell Paris. You can say what you like about Hitler ...

3 It's a segment of the Iraqi supergun thing. A great big gun. Grow up!

4 It's the X chromosome. Not a pork scratching.

5 A pork scratching. Calm your fevered imaginations, you filthy lot!

92 Quiz Shows

What better to answer questions about than the asking of questions? A momentary chance for this book to disappear up its own jacksie/engage in post-modern meta-analysis, you choose.

1 Chris Tarrant asks you if you're confident, whether you want to ask the audience, phone a friend or go fifty-fifty, the scary music plays and all that. *Who Wants to be a Millionaire* is without a doubt one of the all-time classic mega blockbuster quiz shows of all time. Who won the first million here in the UK?

2 Nicholas Parsons has had a wide and varied career, and somehow kept it all going and not been out of work for some nine centuries (I think.) But at one point he did an eleven-year stretch hosting a show where the contestants started off with the grand stake of £15 and played for £1, £3 and £5 points. Its catchphrase was 'And now, live from Norwich, it's the quiz of the week.' What was it?

3 These immortal words signalled time to down tools and enjoy which after-lunch game show?

> 'The heat is on, the time is right,
> It's time for you, for you to play the game . . .'

4 Vernon Kay hosts *All Star Family Fortunes*, the show where we get to see what celebrities' relatives look like, and how thick they are. It's a stalker's dream, as you can fill in all the family blanks, can't you? What is the weirdly named new game show he is hosting, combining physical stuff and questions?

5 What was the name of Channel 5's quiz show that started the same day Channel 5 did (though has long since stopped, thank Christ) that was billed as the 'game show without a host' even though there was a bloke asking the questions in a voiceover, so really he was the host, but they had to have a gimmick?

(Answers on page 212)

Inspiration Corner: Sir Winston Churchill

*'I have taken more out of alcohol
than alcohol has taken out of me.'*
Sir Winston Churchill

If your pub-quiz team is struggling and you feel like you are going to lose, pause to reflect and take some inspiration from the one of the world's greatest masterminds and drinkers, Sir Winston Churchill.

As we know, booze gives you knowledge. But don't forget it also gives you courage. Not Dutch courage – there is after all no such thing, they crumbled in the Boer war (and no one has heard from them since). No, it's just courage, plain and simple. Think about it, you'd have never sent that text or Facebook message had you not been on the sauce all night. And you'd have never tried scaling that rather high perimeter fence after nicking her underwear off the clothes line without that bottle of whisky inside you. (Some would say you wouldn't have stolen the underwear either but that's debatable, and besides, what happened happened.)

So it only makes sense that the most courageous man ever born liked a drink or two. In fact I would say that Churchill was as good at drinking as he was at winning wars. And it's no coincidence that Adolf Hitler was teetotal. Look what happened to him. (If he'd had a couple of pints, he'd have never committed the ultimate act of cowardice; growing a moustache and then not catching Guinness froth in it. A tragic waste.)

Old Churchy's drinking was quite legendary. Some say he was an alcoholic, but I don't believe there is such a thing. A publican's friend, yes; a man with a season ticket to life's booze bus, yes; but an alcoholic, no. He liked sherry in the morning. Personally I prefer Baileys on my cereal for breakfast (it's like milk), but each to their own, I'm not going to question the greatest man ever born and nor should you. He liked beer for lunch and whisky in the evening. Sounds about right. And notice there are no fruit-based drinks in that day of booze.

So remember, when your back is against the ropes and your team is in second to last place, don't give up, don't surrender and never ever run away. Why? Because Winston said so …

'One does not leave a convivial party before closing time.'
Sir Winston Churchill

Answers

1 Judith Keppel back in November 2000. When a million was worth winning too.

2 *Sale of the Century*. Because how much you could win on a game show was capped, the value of the top prize car meant you were up for winning a Lada. Thanks a lot Nicholas!

3 *Going For Gold*. Nine years they squeezed out of that particular lemon.

4 *The Whole 19 Yards*. They've called it that in the hope no one notices they've disembowelled a well-known saying.

5 *100%*. No me either.

93 Soaps

It is obligatory to have a soaps round in one of these quiz books. It's a tragedy really, the way TV used to be about the *Play for Today* and all that and now it's just soap. But then I guess that reflects our national decline – not so long ago we were a world power standing astride the globe, now we're like some pensioner fretting over her allowance and her noisy neighbours – we've gone from drama to soap in two generations. Right, now I've got that off my chest, here's some questions about the opium for the masses now the churches are empty.

1 *Coronation Street* has been running since time began, and when you go Up North everyone is just like that, honest. Apart from Scousers who are just like the people in *Brookside*. It started off with the story of Ken Barlow who'd got a place at university and was embarrassed about his background. How many episodes were originally commissioned?

2 At one point we didn't have enough drivel on our airwaves so we decided to import some from Australia. One of these soaps was directly based on *Coronation Street* and was nearly canned the moment it started. Unfortunately for everyone it was revived by a rival network. Obviously I'm talking about *Neighbours*, I'm not going to ask you that. Which underpant-related company produced it?

3 The Grundys are a family in if-I-hear-it-again-so-help-me-God-I'll-destroy-that-radio-with-a-cricket-bat longest-running soap in all genres that should have been canned many aeons ago *The Archers*. Who did actor Norman Painting play from 1950 until his death on 29 October 2009? He even wrote some episodes.

4 Which mercifully cancelled nineties soap series ended with the line 'You can't trust anyone these days, can you?'

5 *Hollyoaks* is set in and around the fictional Chester suburb of Hollyoaks and is centred around a local higher-education college called Hollyoaks Community College, with the characters generally being in their late teens or early twenties. That's all very well, but have I ever seen *Hollyoaks*?

Answers

1 Just thirteen. Imagine if they'd simply stopped after that. Then this would be a question about one the shortest-running soaps ever. Ah well.

2 Grundy Television.

3 Phil Archer. I guess he must have stopped worrying about typecasting somewhere along the line.

4 *Eldorado*. Can't say I watched any of it, so I'd have been guessing that one, just like you lot.

5 Of course not. And if your whole team is similarly clean, well done, you win a bonus point for remaining uncontaminated.

94 Alright then, *Star Trek* and *Doctor Who* and other nerd bollocks

Well, we're nearly at the end of this book, and so that means we're near the end of our tether, and in the spirit of good nerd/human relations here's a round that should, with any luck, shut them up. Or if not, give them something useful to do, how about that?

1 *Doctor Who*: when *Doctor Who* first aired in 1963 the whole idea was to give kids a sense of history through an entertaining show blah blah blah. But what historic event occurred the night before it debuted?

2 *Star Trek* is top-drawer stuff, particularly Captain Kirk's attitude to exploration – punching the locals in the face, snogging their women, killing them if necessary, and sometimes if not. But it wasn't always going to be Captain Kirk – what was the name of the original Captain of the Enterprise (who cropped up later in the show)?

3 *Star Trek: TheNext Generation* was that one with the bald fella from *Extras* in it. And the Klingon with the big face. And the engineer with the Alice band on his face. And the android fella who wanted to be human. What were their names? All four for one point.

4 *Doctor Who*: the Doctor had a robot dog for a while, called K-9. Brilliant that. See what they did there? K-9. Classic. Which Doctor did K-9 go walkies with? See what I did there? Brilliant eh?

5 *Star Wars* is confusing: the first film is the fourth film, the last film is the third film, and besides, none of them makes any sense – if Darth Vader built C3PO like in the later/earlier film, why do neither of them know? Bollocks, frankly. What is the subtitle of the first film that is the fourth film?

Answers

1 The assassination of President John F. 'JFK' Kennedy. Old nerds claim to be able to remember where they were when they first saw *Doctor Who*, unlike the usual sixties bores who crap on about how they remember where they were when they heard Kennedy was killed. They're as boring as each other, there's really nothing in it.

2 Captain Christopher Pike. If your team got that you are in the company of a nerd.

3 This is nerd porn – Jean-Luc Picard, Worf, Geordi La Forge and Data.

4 The fourth one, Tom Baker, and the tenth one, Dave Tennant. Knowing that kind of stuff is taking up valuable space in your brain, believe me. I mean, you're obviously bright, you can remember obscure stuff, so why not join the army and do something useful?

5 'A new hope'. Knowing that is one of the things that is making you so unhappy, making you feel cut off from normal people. Let it go.

95 The Movies of Danny Glover

When they come to write up the history of cinema they won't even give Danny Glover a footnote. But he's top notch, always gives a hundred per cent, and besides, *Predator 2* was on last night and it wasn't anything like as piss-poor as I remember it being. And the reason? Danny Glover, giving one hundred per cent.

1 How many *Lethal Weapon* films has Danny Glover been in? And he's the business in all of them.

2 In *Lethal Weapon* Danny plays a hard-bitten experienced cop in the LAPD who is partnered with maverick-doesn't-play-by-the-book-cop played by Mel Gibson. It's nowhere near as piss-poor as you remember it. And the reason? Danny Glover giving one hundred per cent. What is the name of Mel Gibson's character?

3 In *Lethal Weapon 2* Danny reprises his role as a hard-bitten experienced cop in the LAPD partnered with maverick-doesn't-play-by-the-book cop played by Mel Gibson. It's nowhere near as piss-poor as you remember. And you know why – Danny, doing everything he can with Mel going full tilt. Who played the love interest in this film?

4 In *Lethal Weapon 3* Danny is once again playing the hard-bitten experienced cop partnered with the maverick Mel, though by now you'd think they were kind of over all this and used to it. In all honesty, even with Danny giving it one hundred per cent it's no *Lethal Weapon*. Who plays their hilarious sidekick Leo Getz?

5 In *Lethal Weapon 4* – well, you know the drill by now – Danny and Mel are still at it. Who plays Mel's girlfriend in it? I expect you don't know, and the reason you don't remember is because the whole time you were thinking stone me, one man is holding this thing together and it's Danny Glover.

Answers

1 It's four. Four.

2 Detective Martin Riggs. He doesn't play by the rules, he's just out there.

3 Patsy Kensit. She's meant to be South African in that film. But to be honest it doesn't matter. Ouch.

4 Joe Pesci, giving it one hundred per cent as an annoying sort of man, yelling at all the people around him.

5 Rene Russo. Yeah me either. She was in that thing with James Bond with the paintings.

96 Cars, Motors, Wheels

'I like driving in my car, honk honk beep beep honk honk squawk! It's not quite a Jaguar' sang Suggs from Madness. They don't write them like that any more. Although actually they didn't write them like that before then either, it was a one-off. But everyone loves their cars, and if I could just remember which lockup mine was in I'd be tooling around town in it right now, not doing this pub quiz. It's a Daimler Sovereign, with 180,000 miles on the clock. Not sure but I think it's a cut and shut. Anyway, what do you know about motors?

1 Which motor manufacturer is famous for its April Fool pranks in the newspapers every year, which have everyone splitting their sides, believe me?

2 The Volkswagen Golf is a classic, especially the old Mark I, hot hatchback or what? Doing donuts in one of those in the pub car park should be compulsory for kids these days. They don't know they're born. What was the Mark I Golf known as in America, because they couldn't cope with the idea of a car called a Golf? You'll never get this, it's so mental.

3 Let's just say that British cars in the 70s were amongst the finest the world has ever seen. I'm just saying that. They weren't, they were diabolical. Which car did British Leyland make before the Austin Maestro?

4 Apart from sheer performance, style and all round pizzazz, what do a Porsche 911 and a Hillman Imp have in common?

5 The Mini is an icon of British design and rightly so, especially what with *The Italian Job* and that. With its transverse mounted engine it changed the way cars were designed in an instant. It wasn't called the Mini to start with, what was it called?

Answers

1 It's BMW. And who says the Germans don't have a sense of humour? Well, I do for one.

2 You won't believe it, it was called a Rabbit. Because somehow driving around in a Rabbit is more acceptable than driving around in a Golf.

3 The Maxi. Once you've driven a Maxi you never forget it. Because they were diabolical.

4 Their engine is at the back. Which is not normal – no matter how many cars they do it in it's wrong.

5 The Austin Seven. If someone in your team did a rotten 'You were only supposed to blow the bloody doors off', deduct a point.

97 Famous Misquotes

To be specific, this next round is about things that never got said by people who never said them at a certain time that didn't take place because it was said never and never actually occurred, specifically.

1 Right, an easy one to start with to ease you in to the round about things that never got said by the people that never said them. Which famous fictional crime-busting, heroin-smoking, deerstalker-wearing, top detective never ever said, 'Elementary, my dear Watson'?

2 This next man was the greatest man ever born and he definitely never ever said this. 'I have nothing to offer but blood, sweat and tears.' Who has been misquoted here?

3 Shakespeare was the greatest playwright blah blah and also blah. Well if he was so good, why can no one ever quote his lines properly? Here's an example. From which play does this line not come? 'Alas, poor Yorick! I knew him well.'

4 People love to ruin a good film quote by completely ballsing it up and getting it wrong. Ingrid Bergman's character in which film never said 'Play it again, Sam'?

5 There's nothing like a classic fat and thin double act (Little and Large, Ant and Dec and Eamonn Holmes and his wife whose name escapes me, though she could do so much better frankly, to name but a few). There is, though, none greater than Laurel and Hardy. They are continually misquoted with the line, 'That's another fine mess you've got me into.' What is the correct line?

Answers

1 Sherlock Holmes. This line never appeared in any of Arthur Conan Doyle's books and, seeing as he was fictional, he definitely never said it anyway.

2 Sir Winston Churchill. What he actually said was 'I have nothing to offer but blood, toil, tears and sweat.' Never ever get Churchill wrong, it's simply too important.

3 *Hamlet*. The actual line was 'Alas, poor Yorick! I knew him, Horatio – a fellow of infinite jest, of most excellent fancy.' The last bit sounds a bit fruity to me, which why people leave it out. Shakespeare also wrote 'All the world's a stage/And all the men and women merely players', which is bang out of order, I'm not some sort of acting poof.

4 *Casablanca*. The proper line is 'Play it once, Sam. For old times' sake. Play it, Sam. Play "As Time Goes By"'.

5 'Well, here's another nice mess you've gotten me into.'

98 France

They're next door, and we don't like them. But that's OK, they're not all that fond of us. But when you have a next-door neighbour, you're best off knowing stuff about them – just in case.

1 France is our nearest European neighbour (we don't count Ireland, be reasonable), but because of the genius of design that is the English Channel we don't actually share a border with them. Which eight sorry bastards do actually share a border? All eight for one point.

2 The capital city of France is Paris. When travelling there by the Eurostar train, which station do you get off at, only to feel your heart plunge as you realise you are in Paris?

3 The French love their mineral water – it's as if using a tap is just too easy. Timewasters. What is the name of the large mountain range in the middle of France?

4 We invented the railways, trains and all that. In first. Wherever you go and see a train, say to yourself, we did that, us. The whole world is covered in railway, like British fingerprints. What is the name of the French railways that they copied off us?

5 Napoleon gave us a good run for our money in the Napoleonic Wars (he started it). He crashed around all over Europe for a couple of decades causing everyone trouble and giving us battles to win. Where was he from?

Answers

1 Belgium, Luxembourg, Germany, Switzerland, Italy, Monaco, Spain and Andorra. My heart bleeds for them all.

2 Gare Du Nord. It's just a shame the French don't get off at Waterloo any more. Why did they have to change that? It was so sweet. Another Gordon Brown glaring error, thanks a lot Gordon.

3 The Massif Central. I guess they think by using a no-nonsense name they somehow make up for all the wasted time not using a tap. God help us all.

4 SNCF. Société Nationale des Chemins de Fer Français. It's a society. What's that all about? Mental.

5 Corsica. His family was Italian. And he ended up in charge of Italy. World gone crazy. Thank God we were on hand to deal with it.

99 The Human Bean Body

We've all got one, in the hands of the right person it's a deadly weapon, but you don't need a licence to have one. And it's not like you know how it works, and the doc never has time to see you. And when something goes wrong it's often too embarrassing to talk about it. Poor old Pelé.

1 Being right-handed is normal, let's just get that straight. But these days left-handed people walk the street unimpeded. How many bones are there in your hand? If you've got a doctor on your team, you're laughing. Unless he gets this wrong, in which case never ask him for advice again.

2 So that was your hand, now how many bones are there in your foot? It might be the same number. It might not. As clues go I'll agree that's pretty lousy. If there's a doctor on your team and he gets this wrong you really should start worrying.

3 In the typical human ribcage – and I have to say that as apparently one in 200 people (give or take) has an atypical number of ribs – how many ribs are there? If there's a doctor in your team simply don't believe a word he says right now. He's incompetent. Seven years at medical school and he doesn't know pub-quiz basics. No wonder the NHS is on its knees.

4 We're still on bones: how many bones make up the human skull? And it's not like you can count them like ribs. That doctor is guessing now.

5 What's the largest bone in the human body? No filth please.

Answers

1 There's twenty-seven. Amazing innit? Your wrist is eight; the metacarpals or palm is five; the other fourteen are your fingers and thumb.

2 There's twenty-six. One less than your hand.

3 There's twenty-four.

4 It's twenty-two, which is weird as it feels like, well, your head bone and your jawbone. There's twenty whole bones in there, hiding.

5 It's the femur or thighbone.

100 Greatest Drinkers

Time to celebrate history's greatest drinkers in a round I like to call Greatest Drinkers, mainly because it's about the greatest drinkers. A celebration of life's most skilled and practiced publican's friends.

1 Keith Moon, it's fair to say, only loved one thing more than using sticks of dynamite to blow up hotel toilets, and that was the booze. His most famous grog-fuelled stunt was driving which type of car into a swimming pool?

2 Ollie Reed too loved his booze, so much so he died for his art. After arm-wrestling and beating five sailors in a bar in Malta, he fell off his bar stool and expired from a heart attack. Which movie was Oliver Reed filming at the time?

3 Which famous drinker uttered these words to the MP Bessie Braddock after she commented on the state of him after a good session on the sauce? 'Bessie, my dear, you are ugly, and what's more, you are disgustingly ugly. But tomorrow I shall be sober and you will still be disgustingly ugly'.

4 Welsh drunk and sometime writer Dylan Thomas loved whole days on the muck and his favoured tipple was gallons of whisky. How old was he when the booze took him from this mortal coil?

5 Final question now in the Greatest Drinkers round. All these people share one thing in common, so what links all these drinkers?

Answers

1 Rolls-Royce. Of course it was a beautiful British motor for a beautiful British boozer. Mind you, some say it was a Cadillac, others a Lincoln Continental. So you can have any of those, the whole thing's shrouded in boozy mystery.

2 *Gladiator*. For an extra bonus point, detail his last round in full.

ANSWER Eight lagers, twelve double rums and half a bottle of whisky. Or, as he called it, breakfast.

3 Sir Winston Churchill. He too was rather ugly, to be fair, but you're not going to argue with him are you?

ANSWER No.

4 Thirty-nine years old. Good innings.

5 No smartarse, it's not that they're all dead, it's that they were all British. Of course they were, they were all good bar dryers.

The Winner Takes It All ...

You've made it through the evening, you've done your best, and with any luck it's brought you fame, glory and a frozen chicken. Or if you're the runnerup, some sausages. You might be wondering how you're going to get the chicken home as it thaws, but you won the quiz, you're the smartest people in the room, you'll figure it out. Maybe you planned ahead and brought a plastic bag. If so, bravo, well done, give yourself a biscuit. If you didn't win, at least console yourself that you have learned more stuff than you knew before, more stuff for next time, more stuff to enrich your life through the power of learning. Because that is the true marvel of the pub quiz, its real gift to humanity and the world, is that it's A University For The Common Man.

That's right, A University For The Common Man, for along with inventing the greatest form of boozing entertainment (though the Zulu drinking game in my first book is, naturally, a close second'), the people who invented the pub quiz created a living fulcrum for the dissemination of knowledge, a place where minds could meet, interact, share and enjoy a pint all at once. When I host a pub quiz I ain't no la-di-da blinking prof giving a lecture, I am not someone with letters after my name (no, my name is over a door, that's all, and that's plenty for me), I am not a boffin with a head full of algebra, no, I am but a humbil publican, yet I am spreading knowledge and facts amongst exactly the sort of people university is aimed at.

After all, if you consider how students spend their time, they spend it either in a lecture or in the bar. So the pub quiz, by the genius of its creator, kills two birds with one stone and combines both – learning and boozing. It's a common sense double whammy. Much more efficient, and in these austere times something those in government could perhaps bear in

---

* The paperback is still out there

mind. Close down the universities and get more publicans to host more pub quizzes and you've saved billions and, more importantly, rescued the British pub. And instead of pissing away three years of taxpayers' loan money, the students could get a job (and a haircut) during the day, attend the pub quiz in the evening, and get a factual skinful.

Radical times call for radical measures, but I know you agree there's something in it. But right now you should pat yourself on the back and congratulate yourself for taking part in the greatest educational institution in the world, the British Pub Quiz.

Picture Credits

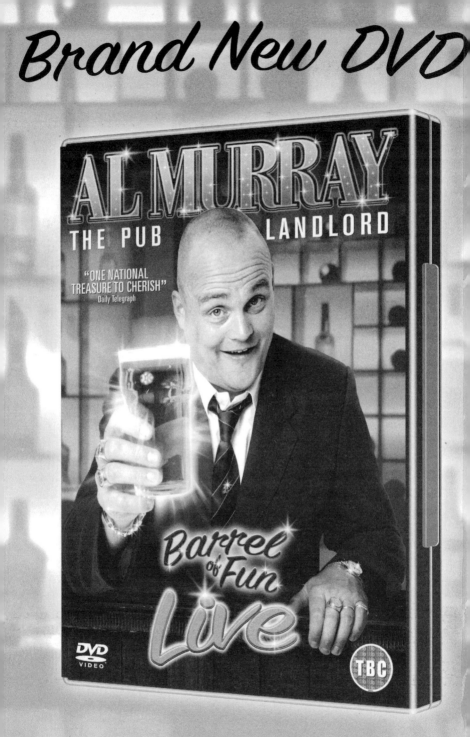